Translating India

The Cultural Politics of English

Rita Kothari

Routledge
Taylor & Francis Group

LONDON AND NEW YORK

First published 2003 by St. Jerome Publishing

Published 2014 by Routledge
2 Park Square, Milton Park, Abingdon, Oxon OX14 4RN
711 Third Avenue, New York, NY 10017, USA

Routledge is an imprint of the Taylor & Francis Group, an informa business

ISBN 13: 978-1-900650-62-5 (pbk)

Cover design by
Steve Fieldhouse, Oldham, UK

Typeset by
Delta Typesetters, Cairo, Egypt

British Library Cataloguing in Publication Data
A catalogue record of this book is available from the British Library

Library of Congress Cataloging-in-Publication Data
Kothari, Rita, 1969-
 Translating India / Rita Kothari.
     p. cm.
Includes bibliographical references and index.
 ISBN 1-900650-62-2 (pbk. : alk. paper)
 1. English language--India. 2. Indic literature--Translations into
English--History and criticism. 3. Indic literature (English)--History
and criticism. 4. India--Languages--Translating into English. 5.
Gujarati language--Translating into English. 6. Translating and
interpreting--India. 7. Languages in contact--India. 8.
Bilingualism--India. I. Title.
 PE3502.I6K67 2003
 428'.0291471--dc21

                        2003008848

Contents

Acknowledgements

This book has taken me to many people of various disciplines, publishers in various cities and friends in many universities – to all these I owe gratitude. I must especially mention Vai Ramanathan-Abbott (University of Davis), Shama Futehally (National School of Drama), Mini Krishnan (Oxford University Press), Achyut Yagnik (Setu, Gujarat), Shuchi Kothari and Nabeel Zuberi (University of Auckland). My young friend Judith Nazareth edited this book, a big thank you, Judy. My colleagues Suguna Ramanathan, Sarvar Sherry Chand and Fr . Francis Parmar have been helpful in more ways than I can describe, and Robert J.C.Young's contribution is also of a similar order.

I have greatly enjoyed working with Mona and Ken Baker Mona Baker's courage and ideological commitment makes me feel proud of my association with St. Jerome.

The support of my two families, Kotharis in Ahmedabad and Makhijas in Mumbai, can only be acknowledged in silent, wordless ways. Abhijit and Shamini patiently put up with my self-absorption – to those two I dedicate *Translating India.*

1. Introduction

> How does a common 'idea of India' make itself available to a Bengali, a Kannadiga, or a speaker of Metei? Only through translation. (Nair, 2002:7)

There comes a point in time when words leap out of their conventional boundaries and embrace different shades of meaning. Something similar has happened to the word "translation", which, long ago meant a linguistic substitution of meaning from a Source Language (SL) into a Target Language (TL) (Catford, 1965). Today it stands as a fundamental principle describing just about any interaction between two languages, cultures or objects. John Sturrock (1990:996) notes:

> In some quarters, ethnography has come to be seen as specifically concerned, no longer with the disingenuous description of other cultures, but with their "translation" into a form comprehensible to our selves. As explicit "translation" of an alien society's customs, rites and beliefs is no longer mistakable for the "real" thing, it is a version or account of another culture familiarized for us through the agency of a translator/ethnographer.

If Sturrock (1990) and Talal Asad (1986) see ethnography as an act of translation, Tejaswini Niranjana (1992) and Eric Cheyfitz (1991) employ it as a metaphor of the Empire. Their postcolonial writings focus on understanding inequalities and slippages in colonial relationships through translation. Homi Bhabha (1994) and Salman Rushdie (1991), on the other hand, seek to articulate hybrid intercultural spaces and identities through the term 'translation' – Rushdie refers to his tribe as "translated men"(1991: 17). Looking at this widening rubric, it is clear that "our perception of translation has changed profoundly in the last decade or so" (Holmstrom, 1997:4-5). What is now acknowledged is that the translation process is one in which we tentatively and precariously arrive at meanings of one cultural context and re-inscribe them, however inadequately, in another. If, as cultural theorists suggest, culture is the silent language that members of a specific ethnic, racial or cultural group understand, entering cultures involves translating this language along with its grammar, syntax and metaphors. It should also be noted that the terms 'translation' and 'metaphor' both share the similar connotation of 'carrying across' or 'transferring' through their etymology. Translation serves as any metaphor of understanding the 'other' and metaphor itself acquires a sense of translation. This synonymity between 'metaphor' and 'translation' takes the definition of translation into the realms of the infinite, hence the need to set a provisional limit on this term and clarify how it is being used in this book.

Translating India is centred on the production of the body referred to as Indian Literature in English translation (hereafter ILET). It concerns itself with this industry and what goes into feeding it. It is also interested in the quarters that give this industry its present prominence and help sustain its energy. The frenetic activity of ILET in the last two decades, its unprecedented rise from being a marginal event to a pervasive trend begs attention. In fact, the existence of ILET as a body which is substantial and distinct is itself a recent phenomenon. ILET has been an ancillary activity of Indian Writing in English (hereafter IWE) confused with and being subsumed into the body of IWE.[1] For a long time, ILET was neither significant nor voluminous enough to draw attention to itself as a separate body. The first recognition of Indian literature in English translation as a body distinct from Indian Writing in English came when Gokak stated, "one of the befitting ways of honouring the message and significance of *Gitanjali* is to create a body of Indo-English writing, which will wear *Gitanjali* as a jewel in its crown" (1964:166). Later in the early eighties in a pioneering study *Translation as Discovery*, Sujit Mukherjee used Gokak's taxonomy to map the scope of 'Indo-English' referring to what is now called Indian Literature in English translation or 'regional' literatures in translation.[2] This does not mean, however, that translating into English is a recent activity. The chapter titled "Recalling: English Translation in Colonial India" in this book shows how the origins of English translations in India go back to the nineteenth century. At the same time, translations in English were few and far between until almost the middle of the sixties. After India's political independence in 1947, the ambiguous and controversial position of English did not provide an atmosphere conducive for both 'original' as well translated works in English. The independent state conveyed its first gesture of patronage towards creative writing in English by conferring the Sahitya Akademi award on R.K. Narayan in 1965. All was still not well with writing in English, however, creative writing in English continued amidst allegations and defences. Translation activity in English was particularly meagre, thanks to prejudices against translations in general and English translations of Indian literature in particular. Given this background of marginality, the dramatic rise of translations that are produced, read, absorbed in curricula today appears staggering. The contexts surrounding this shift are at the heart of *Translating India*. The six chapters of this book represent various quarters that provide consensus and fuel to ILET.

---

[1] See my "The Elephant and the Ant: Indian Literature in English/Translation" for an analysis of the historical and contested relationship between literature produced in English and literature translated into English in India. Critical Practice, January 2003, Issue No. 17.

[2] It is important to clarify here the connotations of loaded terms like 'Indian literature' and 'regional literature. The two are not interchangeable. The assumption behind 'regional literature' is that it represents a region, a space and only some languages in India have 'regions'. I have, however, included within the ambit of 'regional literature' even those languages which are not defined by 'regions' and which have therefore considerably less infrastructural support. The much-contested baggy term 'Indian literature' justifies its inclusion in this study because it facilitates discussions which would otherwise be bogged down by the minutiae of clarifications.

As was mentioned earlier, the first chapter "Recalling" provides a thematic overview of English translations as carried out by the East India officers and/or white Orientalists scholars of the nineteenth century. Once Indian subjects entered into polemical debates with the British on the latter's version of Hinduism and of the Indian epics and conflicting perceptions of the past, for the first time we find English translations by Indians. The ideologies underlying both acts are of interest to us since as Indian translators we carry out a resistant and/or assimilative dialogue with the West through translation even today. The chapter "Two Worlds Theory" draws a map of India's linguistic economy in the years after Independence and situates 'modern' Indian languages (as opposed to an elite and pan-Indian language like Sanskrit) and the English language in their emerging configurations.[3] The English language remains a leitmotif all the way from the Nehruvian vision of the nation in the fifties and sixties to a post-liberalised India of the nineties so that despite conflicting political and economic ideologies, its position remains unchallenged. At the same time, English in postcolonial India is in a new avatar and different things are expected of it. The chapter "Two Worlds Theory" highlights English's reconfigured relationship with the Indian languages and how it provides a condition for accommodating translation.

The Indian 'middle class' inhabits a bilingual space of language and worldview and translation is one of the manifestations of this phenomenon. Expressions, icons and symbols satisfying this need in the middle class to produce and receive 'local' and 'global' ways of living life sell easily in India today. The chapter "Outside the Discipline Machine" forges connections between the symbiotic relationship between the middle class and the English language and locates English translation there.

Translating India straddles the specialized and the general sphere of English translation in India. It is interested in a hypothetical situation of why a nameless, faceless, English-reading person in middle-town visits a bookshop and picks up a work in translation. It is equally interested in why students or teachers of sociology or 'English literature' read works in translation and the uses they put them to. These questions are concerned with readerships and layered segments within Indian readerships. Although they appear tenuously linked with the subject of translation, they throw light on the literary as well as paraliterary forces that make translations work in ways that have never worked before. Both "Within Academia" and "Outside the Discipline Machine" are reflections on these forces, the canons that absorb texts in translation and the social needs that translation implicitly professes to fulfill. In short, the twin chapters address the issue of socio-cultural viability of English translation in India. The word 'viability' is very crucial in economic contexts and a text in

---

[3] E.V. Ramakrishnan (1997) provides a succinct summation of the "tripartite language system" of India with its three layers of pan-Indian traditional elite language like Sanskrit; pan-Indian modern language like English and other Indian languages. According to him, the three are assumed to represent the ethos of tradition, modernity and everydayness.

translation is a literary as well as an economic product that must sell by the end of the day. Of course this commercial concern shifts in emphases from publisher to publisher, and takes almost tertiary place with institutions of 'nation-building' such as the Sahitya Akademi and the National Book Trust. The chapter "Publishers' Perspective" examines the role of the publishing industry, its perception of the translation activity and the small and big ways in which it impacts the body of ILET. The publication of slow-moving books (as opposed to 'bestsellers' or even textbooks), especially translations, is far from lucrative in business terms. At the same time, translation titles now seem to find a place in the publishing lists of most commercial and non-commercial publishers. It is useful to inquire into the perceptions of translation activity that lead publishers to invest time and money in this activity; and the criteria and philosophy governing the choice of texts. Has the publication of texts in translation become economically viable now? Does it also mean that there are better and more competent translators in the country than before? Is the publishing industry responding to a latent market that always existed, or is it by making resources available, creating a market? There are no clear-cut answers to these questions. However, through interviews with publishers or editors directly involved in this activity, I have explored some of these areas.

I have offered historical, disciplinary, economic and sociological contexts that may 'explain' the rise of the English translation, without implying, of course, a cause-and-effect relationship. The contexts impinging, affecting and governing ILET at the 'national' level have slightly different enactments in the 'regional' arenas. Hence when we examine the production of a specific 'regional' literature in English translation, the focus shifts from the general to the particular and throws light on both processes. In order to substantiate, I have, in the final chapter , taken the case of Gujarati literature in English translation. The history of Gujarat's relationship with the English language has been a chequered one, a phenomenon reflected in the near-total absence of English writing as well as translations by Gujaratis until recently. The long-standing Gandhian tradition, which mitigated an anglicized outlook, combined with a mercantile outlook of the community to make Gujarat's response to colonialism and the colonial language an interesting one. Furthermore, Gujarat is also one of the most urbanized states in the country and its language figures as one of the 'major' languages in the Constitution. The lack of translations from Gujarat not only reflect Gujarati's inability or unwillingness to translate or trade with English, but also reflects the politics of translation activity at large. What self-perceptions underlie a community's decision to translate its literature and 'represent'? What is representation all about and has Gujarat also finally been scrambling for one? Translation is a site of a community's unspoken desires and anxieties, and different languages in India have different narratives of translation to tell. This is only one such narrative.

"We are poised at an interesting point. There is a ferment; when it subsides, we'll have to take stock of what's left" (Davidar in Paranjpe:1992). Although these words refer to the Indian English novel, they hold relevance for Indian literature (especially fiction) in translation also. The production, reception and canonization of English texts in translation are fledgling and nebulous activities. In my attempt to capture this flux, and confine it within academic bounds many things remain unattended to which I shall turn later. For the moment, a few words about the methodology of this book are in order. The six chapters in this book derive unity by proceeding from the same premise of why translating into English appears to be a possible, desirable, or even a necessary activity? The first chapter highlights ideologies that underlay translation in the past and it engages in a thematic overview for its purposes. The second chapter takes recourse to historical and socio linguistics to point out an increasing condition of bilingualism and biculturalism. The twin chapters on literary/academic and para-literary contexts draw parallels with audio and visual phenomena and make use of newspaper articles, reviews, prefaces and blurbs to show how translations are 'framed' by publishers and reader consumers. The chapter on the publishing industry and the case-study of Gujarati rely heavily on oral interviews with publishers and editors in the former and Gujarati teachers and intellectuals in the latter.

Finally, it must be stated that *Translating India* is not about the act, but the activity of translation and the conditions under which it gains momentum and unanimous approval. Styles of translation are not unrelated to the central argument of this book, but they do not enjoy as much premium as they do in traditional scholarship on translation. This book takes issue with a view that literary products 'reflect' or 'mirror' external reality and establishes that literary products are tethered to material realities in many mundane ways and that it is impossible to disconnect literary from the para-literary.

2.   Recalling: English Translations in Colonial India

> Translation is stigmatized as a form of writing, discouraged by copyright law, depreciated by the academy, exploited by publishers and corporations, governments and religious organizations. (Venuti, 1998:1)

The Sahitya Akademi (a semi-government publishing house) which had not included English as one of its scheduled languages until the sixties, awarded a Translation Prize for English in the eighties. In the nineties, Katha (a non-profit private publishing house) began as an organization solely concerned with translation and instituted the A.K. Ramanujan Award for translation. In 2000, the Crossword chain of bookshops in India included English translations in their short-list. In the last few years there have been on an average at least five national seminars on translation in India. Courses on translation studies and Indian literature in English translation are taught in about twenty universities. Both Penguin and Picador India launched their operations in India with a decision to tap the Indian market for books written in, and translated into English. The rise in the institutionalization through awards and courses in India has also coincided with energetic and radical debates on translation in India and the West. These debates stridently question the very assumption of the 'original' let alone its superiority over a translation. Given this nature of hectic activity, Venuti's stern conclusion about the state of translation seems paradoxical, especially when we look at the Indian situation. Yet what needs to be noted is that the degree of attention and glamour that the developments enumerated above suggest, are unique only to *English* translation activity in India. The rise in the visibility and acceptance of ILET in the last two decades begs attention. I have tried to identify the quarters from which it has received consensus and study the interconnections.

When compared with translations from Indian languages into other Indian languages (intra-Indian), a much older activity, the importance attached to English translation appears quite disproportionate. At the same time, when certain literary forms acquire prominence at specific points in history, there is a range of tangible and intangible determinants at work. The issues surrounding the privileged position of English translation in India will be explored later. For now, we turn briefly to the scenario of intra-Indian translations.

Phenomenon: Old and New

Given India's multilingualism, most Indians straddle at least two languages in their everyday lives. This is an informal and unstudied part of daily life in India. A historical perspective of Indian translation activity in general requires consideration in terms of three stages: oral, written and printed. There is, of course, no mechanism for tracing the oral tradition of translation. The written tradition, on the other hand, is rooted in medieval India, around the fourteenth and fifteen centuries, when excerpts from the Sanskrit scriptures began to travel into the 'regional' languages. Jnaneshwara's translation of the *Bhagawad-Gita* (called *Jnaneswari* in Marathi) and the various (sub)versions of the *Ramayana* and the *Mahabharata* in different languages are a part of this written tradition. The journey made from the exalted Sanskrit scriptures to the more humble *'desi'* languages was symptomatic of a quiet spiritual revolution made possible through translation, as the previously inaccessible scriptures became available to the unprivileged, lower classes. This phenomenon is to be found in languages as geographically distant as Gujarati and Assamese, Malayalam and Hindi. In that sense, the nature of outflow from Sanskrit into Indian languages is analogous to the West's movement from Latin to Vulgate. It was an attempt to release scriptures "from the monopolist custody of Sanskrit pundits" (Bassnett and Trivedi, 1999:10) and move towards greater secularization and vernacularism. The analogy of translation between West and India cannot be stretched beyond this point. Unlike the Bible translation and the paradigms set therein, the Indian mode of translating was never resolutely faithful. As the editors of *Postcolonial Translation* point out:

> Thus, 'imitation' in the neo-classical sense was in India a form of translation as being a repetition of something already written, and formed the staple of the pre-colonial literary tradition with those two great source-books of Indian culture, the *Ramayana* and the *Mahabharata*, being worked and reworked by countless writers in Sanskrit itself as well as in all the modern Indian languages, with various shifts of emphasis and ideology through which gaps in the original were inventively filled in, silences were rendered poignantly articulate, and even some of the great heroes turned into villains and villains into heroes. (ibid:9)

At the heart of this 'liberal' attitude is perhaps the relationship between Sanskrit and the 'regional' languages. While Sanskrit enjoyed an elitist and central position compared to other Indian languages, it could still be claimed as a part of the Hindu inheritance. Translating from Sanskrit was a matter of both deference and courage; translators adulated Sanskrit but also displayed intimacy and freedom in the act of translation. Therefore these "translations in vernaculars were hardly passive cultural creations; and they gradually produced an alternative literature which told the same stories with subtle emphases to alternative audiences" (Kaviraj, 1992:35). This medieval tradition of translation was interrupted, modified and systematized in the colonial phase of India's history, a matter discussed elsewhere in this study.

To come back to Venuti, the marginalization of translations he points to has a temporal dimension. It stems from capitalistic notions of 'copyright' and 'ownership'. The advent of printing in Europe after the fifteenth century, and in India after 1800, is integrally connected with the status of a translator. The translator has remained 'invisible' (see Venuti, 1995) in all capitalist countries. The notion of the 'original' as superior lies at the heart of this invisibility. As the editors of *Postcolonial Translation* note:

> ... the concept of the high status original is a relatively recent phenomenon. Medieval writer and/or translators were not troubled by this phantasm. It arose as a result of the invention of printing and the spread of literacy, linked to the emergence of the idea of an author as 'owner' of his or her text. (Bassnett and Trivedi, 1999:2)

Venuti encapsulates a very modern situation of print-capitalism which thrives on translation, but hardly ever acknowledges its debt. While the tyranny of the original is a truth that cannot be gainsaid, some languages fare better as TLs than others. Indian English literature has a less central place compared to English literature. At the same time, English is emerging as the most desirable choice as TL and the body of English translations in India is privileged over translations into other Indian languages. What gives English this legitimacy? How is this consensus formed and sustained? How do various institutions – public and private, educational and cultural – contribute to the more or less unanimous point of view that English translations of Indian texts are indispensable? The following discussion undertakes a thematic overview of English translation activity in India.

The selection and methodology of the historiography of English translation activity in India that follows requires some clarification. I have attempted to map the origins and development of translations from Indian languages into English and do not claim to give a comprehensive account of all translations from Indian languages into English. Rather, I have offered a selective overview of some translations that serve as milestones, and have been significant in altering the structures of source and target cultures; in other words, shaping the 'field' in a significant way. In mapping these translations and their contexts, the choice of texts is not based upon any fixed criterion of 'most representative' or 'most popular'. I have, by and large, selected texts that lend themselves to an investigation of the processes and contexts behind their emergence and highlight the complex nature of translation into English. 'Texts' in this sense serve as icons, the concern being with what they stand for rather than what they are. The methods employed to highlight the agenda and purpose of translations is not textual; there is no attempt to compare a translation with its 'original'. I have, instead, tried to read *around* the act of translation and looked at the 'outwork' – the reasons for the inception of a certain text, the translator's background and her relationship vis-à-vis her audience. Special attention, therefore, has been paid to prefaces, introductions or notes that frame and cite the 'main text' for 'historical' readers. Anitha Devasia and Susie Tharu state that prefaces:

> ... stake out the border-lines between work and world, granting the author momentary respite from the disciplines of the text. In a brief appearance

front stage before the curtain is raised, authors may appear unaccustomed to play their everyday selves and engage in a direct and autobiographical mode of address. (1995:5)

In addition to prefaces, readers' responses (wherever possible) from both source and target cultures have been used as indices of the reception of specific texts.

Knowing the Orient

The English language came to India, and from the 18th century onwards, gave clear signs of wanting to stay on. One clear sign or signal was through acts of translation (Mukherjee S. 1997:150). Translations from Indian languages into English are products of the special context of late eighteenth and nineteenth century British India (see Mukherjee, 1997). The translations initiated in the period of British Orientalism in India provide an enduring account of the construction of knowledge and relationships integral to colonial rule. The period from 1772 to 1840 witnessed multiple systems of knowledge constructed by the British and translations were one outcome of this knowledge-creating enterprise. A series of translations of ancient Indian texts undertaken by the British after 1770, has served for generations (among Indians and Europeans) as an 'authentic' account of India. The Orient was 'translated' and made available for self-definition not only to the Europeans, but also to the Orientals themselves (Inden, 1986:40-46). As such, travel writings, histories and other dictionaries may also be seen as acts of translation – acts of interpreting local systems of signification and translating them into one's own understanding of a dominant culture. However, for reasons of focus, I will restrict the discussion here to the underlying assumptions and ideologies as the British sought to translate Indian legal, religious and literary texts into their own language.

The administrative and cultural preoccupation of the East India Company in the mid-nineteenth century necessitated a more exhaustive attempt at 'knowing the Orient'. This set off a many-sided process in which the British were engaged. Translation was one of the manifestations of this process. In the early days of the colonial encounter, the English set about studying the 'Hindoo' psyche and the ancient texts seemed the most 'logical' way to begin. Reading those texts and making them available for subsequent officers was the first step for the British. This involved translation. It helped unveil the mystique around ancient Indian civilization because "idioms [got] desacralized by the very act of translation" (Majeed, 1992:20). Moreover, Warren Hastings believed that natives had to be ruled by their own principles and institutions. In order to convince people back home of this Orientalist way of administration, a code, a text – in English – was required. The result was an English translation of a legal text, *Vivadarnavsetu* (*Across the sea of litigation*) as *A Code of Gentoo Laws* or *Ordinations of the Pundits* (1776), by Nathaniel Brassey Halhed.

Halhed belonged to the English elite. After a false start as a dramatist and then a "certain emotional disappointment" Halhed took the India assignment "on the rebound" (Kesavan, 1985, I:182). In his days at Christchurch he had come into contact with William Jones and that acquaintance also played an important role in his decision to come to India. Halhed had learnt Persian and Arabic before he learned Sanskrit. Sisir Kumar Das notes how there was a "feeling at that time that a knowledge of Arabic and Persian could unlock the secrets of the Orient" (1991:183). Meanwhile in India, Warren Hastings was trying to deal with the vexing problem of the native legal system. Halhed's arrival in India coincided with Hastings' Judiciary Plan of 1772, a happy coincidence for Halhed who had otherwise failed to make a very successful life back home. Hastings asked Halhed to prepare an English commentary on the legal codes, and an elaborate method of English translation from Sanskrit into Persian and then into English followed. Halhed inaugurated the practice of Indian texts in English translation by laying down, in no unspecific terms, the administrative usefulness of the *Code*:

> The importance of the commerce of India, and the advantages of a territorial establishment in Bengal, have at length awakened the attention of the British Legislature to every circumstance that may conciliate the affections of the natives, or ensure stability to the acquisition. Nothing can so favourably conduce to these two points as a well-timed toleration in matters of religion, and an adoption of such original institutes of the country as do not immediately clash with the laws or interests of the conquerors. (1970:142)

The book was initially meant to be a private edition published by the East India Company. In another two years, not only had pirated and renewed editions of the *Code* appeared, but it had also been translated into French and German. There are various issues regarding the *Code*. Questions can be raised about whether the *Code*, thrice removed from Sanskrit, can be considered a translation proper. William Jones raised doubts about the accuracy of the translation. In a letter dated 19th March 1788, addressed to Cornwallis, Jones states:

> But, whatever be the merit of the original, the translation of it has no authority, and is of no other use than to suggest inquiries on the many dark passages, which we find in it: properly speaking, indeed, we cannot call it a translation; for though Mr. Halhed performed his part with fidelity, yet the Persian interpreter had supplied him only with a loose injudicious epitome of the original Sanscrit, in which abstract many essential passages are omitted. All this I say with confidence, having already perused no small part of the original with a learned Pandit, comparing it, as I proceeded, with the English version. (1970:797)

Jones mistrusted the Persian interpreter; some others had suspicions about the willingness and commitment of the Brahmins to impart information to Halhed.

However, there were few means of assessing the 'accuracy' of the text because the tradition of Sanskrit studies had yet to be established. The awkwardness of its modus operandi notwithstanding, the final product met with immediate dissemination and sales in Europe. Its reception, however, was far from uniform. To theoretical jurists and historians of civilization the *Code* became the fundamental source on Hindu laws and customs (Rocher, 1983:55). On the other hand, practitioners in courts found the *Code* full of inconsistencies. Mild misdemeanours appeared to call for severe punishment whereas serious crimes led to mild reprimands. This sense of the contradiction added to the general European bewilderment regarding India. The laws served as an index for assessing the level of civilization India had reached. To some it brought home the antiquity and sophistication of thought in Hindu civilization. To detractors like James Mill who quotes copiously from the *Code*, the laws only reinforced their opinion of the savage nature of the Hindus. Mill quotes the following passage from the *Code* to testify despotic and merciless government: "If a man makes complaint before the magistrate against the magistrate's counsellor, without any real fault in him, or performs any business or service for the magistrate's accuser, the magistrate shall put him to death". To this James Mill says, "Under the operation of this law, the magistrate had little to fear from accusation. There could be no remedy for any grievance; because the existence of any grievance could hardly ever be told" (1858:192).

The mixed reception of the *Code* is an indication of the seriousness with which the first work translated into English was taken. Save a few, almost everybody in Europe saw this translation as a reflection of Indian society and its legal system. There is no record, however, of Indian responses to the *Code*. The English translation was very obviously meant for English readers. The Hindu pundits who anthologized the collection of codes were not even aware that there would be an English translation of their work. To Bengali Indians Halhed's name was associated more with the *Grammar of the Bengali Language* than with the *Code*. As Rocher concludes, "All in all the *Code of Gentoo Laws* had more influence as an antiquarian and Indological document than as a book of law, and its impact was greater on Europe than on India" (1983:23). The *Code* had a lasting impact in other ways: it opened up the field of Sanskrit studies for the British, which ultimately led to many translations of Indological texts. According to Cohn, eighteenth century texts including translations, travel writings, surveys, etc. "began the establishment of discursive formation, defined an epistemological space, created a discourse, and had the effect of converting Indian forms of knowledge into European objects" (1996:283). If such is the case, the *Code* stands as one of the texts that initiated the formation of this discourse.

All scattered attempts at learning Sanskrit became organized in Charles Wilkins, the first European translator to translate directly from Sanskrit and prepare a *Grammar of Sanskrit Language*. Studying Wilkins' *Grammar* became a regular feature for all civil servants coming to India. In terms of creating a fine, philosophical other-worldly view of the Orient, Wilkins' translation of the *Geeta* is a landmark. This brings us to another important stage in the history of translations by the British. Wilkins translation of the *Geeta* called *The Bhagvet-Geeta* (1784) marked, in William Jones' opinion, an "event that made it possible for the first time to have a reliable impression of Indian literature" (Drew, 1987:78). This reliability could be claimed by Jones, in light of the seeming absence of marring, impure mediations. On the other hand, unlike Halhed's *Code*, the *Geeta*, had very little practical value. It was perhaps a relatively un-planned by-product of Wilkins' serious engagement with Persian. However, when Warren Hastings read an excerpt of the translated *Geeta*, it seemed to him an ideal means of propaganda to make a case for an Indianized administration. He wrote to Nathaniel Smith, the chairman of the East India Company requesting publication of the translation:

> Every accumulation of the knowledge and especially such as is obtained by social communication with people over whom we exercise a dominion founded on the right of conquest, is useful to the State ...it attracts and conciliates distant affections; it lessens the weight of the chain by which the natives are held in subjection; and it imprints on the hearts of our own countrymen the sense and obligation of benevolence. (1970:189)

To support his cause, Warren Hastings linked an acquisition of any knowledge about the Orient with the acquisition of power for the State. The connection, beyond a point, did become tenuous. In the Preface to his translation of the *Geeta* Wilkins spoke of Hastings' encouragement of the Company's servants "to render themselves more capable of performing their duty ... by the study of the languages, the laws and customs of the natives" (1970:192). It is difficult to say whether the English translation of the *Geeta* rendered the civil servants more capable in discharging their duties. In any case, the appearance of the *Geeta* in English marked an important stage in the development of Western awareness of India. The translation did not bring about any tangible change, but it reaffirmed a picture of a pristine and spiritual Indian past, a time when rituals and superstitious practices had not contaminated the social fabric. The Oriental-ists had acquired a view from various materials that Hinduism in its sublime moments had been deistic and unitary. The Hindus in their state of glory, which was of course in the past, had not engaged in polytheistic practices. The *Geeta* gave a picture of a time when Hinduism was philosophical and non-ritualistic. Polytheism was a feature attributed by the British to India's degenerate present. Wilkins himself says in his preface that the

> ... most learned Brahmans of the present times are Unitarians...but, at the same time that they believe but in one God, an universal spirit, they so far comply with the prejudices of the vulgar, as outwardly to perform all the ceremonies...these ceremonies, are as much the bread of the Brahmans, as

> the superstition of the vulgar is the support of the priesthood in other
> countries. (ibid:194)

Wilkins' translation suited the Western taste for a philosophical and speculative, as opposed to a ritualistic Hinduism. Images of a hallowed past when the 'gymnosophists' of the East discussed mankind's existence, were disseminated. If Halhed's *Code* was Europe's 'key' to India's legal system, Wilkins' *Geeta* was a key to religion in India.

The fact that the *Code* made hardly any impact on Indian audiences has found mention earlier. On the other hand, the central importance accorded to the *Geeta* by its selection for an English translation over many other spiritual texts had a far-reaching impact upon Indian audiences. I do not mean to imply that before Wilkins translated the *Geeta* it was an unimportant text, rather, I would like to emphasize the role translation has played in the 'canonization' of the *Geeta* in the Indian consciousness. It seemed to many Indians that Wilkins' *Geeta* marked an important shift "from a series of travelers' tales" to a time when "the west began not only to make efforts to understand, but value India and her culture" (Kejriwal, 1988:21). The identification and privileging of the *Geeta*, as a primary text by the rulers, had a profound impact upon the ruled. It is not a coincidence that the *Geeta* became the key text for self-definition as leaders from Gandhi to Tilak attempted to articulate an Indian identity.

The most concerted effort regarding the formation of Oriental knowledge through translations came from William Jones. Jones provided, among other things, an academic counterpart to Hastings' administrative concerns. He had read various references to the *Manusmruti* in the process of pursuing his vocation as a judge and realized that it was one of the oldest extant works on law in India. After reading it in the original, Jones felt confident enough to undertake its translation himself. Jones' decision to translate an antiquarian text rather than something more representative of current practice stemmed from a conviction that all usage and manners have an explanation in a 'text' and any accretions of time such as defective, easily available translations corrupt the 'purity' of that text. Translations were important for Jones also because "the apparent monopoly of a form of indigenous knowledge by certain classes could only be broken through translation" (Majeed, 1992:20). The outcome of this is the *Institutes of Hindu Law*; or, *The Ordinances of Menu*, Jones' translation of the *Manusmruti* into English. This translation was highly influential in shaping cultural perceptions and legal systems for Indians. It also paved the path for Jones' *Digest*, a more comprehensive project completed by H.T. Colebrooke.

Jones' translation of the *Manusmruti* went through several editions. Rocher notes that since *Manusmruti* was "translated by the most eminent scholar of Hindu law of his time endowed the *Manusmruti* with a reputation that was to withstand the discovery of other texts, ancient and modern, that were much more useful from a legal standpoint" (1993:229). The editor of the third edition explains elaborately how the translator handled a recalcitrant text with adeptness.

The "peculiarity" of the content of the book, according to him, would "explain the difficulty" the "learned" translator had (Grady, 1869:vi). Jones himself begins his preface by recording Britain's "compliance" (1869:xi) with the maxim that the natives are best ruled with their own laws. The natives, he informs the readers "universally and sincerely believed that all their ancient usages and established rules had the sanction of an actual revelation from heaven…". Then Jones goes on to caution his reader about the "system of despotism and priestcraft" (ibid:xix) contained in the doctrines of the source text and concludes by saying:

> Whatever opinion in short may be formed of Menu and his laws, in a country happily enlightened by sound philosophy and the only true revelation, it must be remembered, that those laws are actually revered, as the word of the Most High, by nations of great importance to the political and commercial interests of Europe, and particularly by many millions of Hindu subjects, whose well directed industry would add largely to the wealth of Britain, and who ask no more in return than protection for their persons and places of abode, justice in their temporal concerns, indulgence to the prejudices of their old religion, and the benefit of those laws, which they have been taught to believe sacred, and which alone they can possibly comprehend". (ibid:xx)

The interlocking of translation as a discursive practice with the imperial project of colonization in this case was quite complete. The choice of text, the ideological underpinnings of the translator's stance, the 'transparency of representation' assumed in the entire exercise – work towards the construction of a colonial subject who lives a-temporally and follows a despotic, peculiar and incomprehensible system. Jones had a penchant for things antique and remote in their history. He declared that in all his inquiries concerning the history of India:

> I shall confine my researches downwards to the Mohammedan conquests
> at the beginning of the eleventh century, but extend them upwards, as high
> as possible, to the earliest records of the human species. (1970:248)

The complete refusal to take cognizance of India's present is evident in Jones' decision to refer to an ancient text for judicial matters of the present. However, the translator's choice is made out to be the natives' wish for usages and practices of a distant past. The 'visible' translator speaks for an 'invisible' native whose well-directed industry will add to the commercial wealth of Britain while the translator's own efforts contribute to cultural gains!

The *Code* and the translation of the *Manusmruti* were harnessed to colonial administration in an obvious way. They were undertaken at government behest and belie the view that the "world of scholarship and the world of administration during this period were worlds apart and not necessarily complementary to each other" (Kejriwal, 1988:226). However, not all translations in this period were undertaken for administrative or political reasons, some acquired a political slant in their use. Like the *Geeta*, Jones' choice of Kalidasa's *Abhignan-shakuntalam* was also somewhat ad hoc. Jones undertook this translation when, as the leading member of the Asiatic Society, he was looking for any 'historical' document that would throw light upon ancient Indian history. The indistinct nature of genres in India, history sliding into myth or turning into fable, was a bewildering phenomenon for the British. Even before he came to India, Jones had heard of a genre called '*natac*' which was said to contain ancient history uncorrupted by fable (Kejriwal, 1988). Later on some Europeans told him that '*natacs*' were discourses on arts and music. Finally, the learned Brahmin Radhakant informed Jones that '*natacs*' were plays, and according to him, the most well known play was *Abhignanshakuntalam*. Jones translated it into English and it evoked a wider response than any other 'document' of that period. Jones' translation of *Abhignanshakuntalam* called *Sakontala* or *The Fatal Ring* in English became both popular and authoritative. It appeared in 1789 and a startled Europe opened its eyes to the East. When the play reached England, it was welcomed and reviewed widely. The responses to the play, whether Goethe in a flamboyant mode or James Mill in a negative mode acknowledge the impact it had on its readers. Mill cites from Jones' translation of the *Manusmruti* the detailed evolution of elements and their properties only to reject them as "absurd ideas" and "random guesses" (1858:85). Although he rejects *Shakuntalam* as unoriginal, he takes the transparency of the translation for granted, thereby investing Jones' effort with authority. *Blackwood's Edinburgh Magazine* wrote in its review of the play:

> Will our readers turn from these fierce, wild and turbulent passions, breathed out from the constantly agitated bosom of European life, as exhibited in the English and German drama ... One flight of the imagination and we find ourselves almost on another earth. It is delightful to sink away into those old green and noiseless sanctuaries, to look on the Brahmins as they pass their whole lives in silent and reverential adoration, – virgins playing with the antelopes and bright-plumaged birds among those gorgeous woods – and, as the scene shifts, to find ourselves amid the old magnificence of oriental cities, or wafted on the chariot of some deity up to the palaces of the sky. (Oct. 1819, Mar. 1820,VI:417)

What needs to be emphasized here is the circulation of idyllic and pastoral images, severed from their social context, that contributed to what Niranjana expresses as "the textualized India to Europe" (1992:42). At the same time, notes G.N. Devy, "Jones was the first British scholar to perceive India in terms of a literary culture and his discovery of India as a nation with a literature, and a literature extending to remote antiquity, enthused his readers in Britain to look to India for literary inspiration" (1998a:78). Translations previous to *Shakuntalam* had exposed the West to the spiritual, philosophical and legal aspects of Indian civilization. Through the translation of *Shakuntalam* Jones introduced the literary side of India to the West. The privileging of *Shakuntalam* in the Western world enabled its creation into a national commodity as far as Indians were concerned. *Shakuntalam* as a text became a marker of India's cultural prestige and one of the 'primary' texts in Indian consciousness. It was translated into more than ten Indian languages in the nineteenth century. In the following century, *Shakuntalam* was translated into Marathi (1861), Hindi (1863), Gujarati (1867, 1875 and 1881), Telugu (1870, 1875 and 1883), Tamil (1876 and 1880) and Bengali (several times).

The British phase of translation into English culminated in Jones' translation of *Shakuntalam*. We must bear in mind that hardly anything, at this time, was translated from other Indian languages. This was one of the manifestations of the Orientalist disregard for India's present. There was a large preponderance of works translated from Sanskrit because Sanskrit was the Ursprache and the only residue of a hallowed past. This point of view led to serious imbalances of representation. Again, within that limited corpus, works of a legal and spiritual nature dominated. A long tradition of highly metaphysical works translated from Sanskrit, says Brough, led the West to believe in the universal mysticism and other-worldliness of ancient India (1968). Imbalances of this nature made the representation of India tilt in a certain direction and we will see in the next section how even Indian translators, were unable to correct this picture for a long time.

The Indian Intervention

Nineteenth-century colonial India was marked by a decline of Orientalist activities, at least among the British scholars. Translations into English by the English were few and far between. The Germans, however, carried on with that tradition more regularly. Without implying a strict cause and effect relationship, this floundering of activity can be understood in the following terms: The Romantic revolution even in Britain had came to an end and there were few takers for transcendentalism. Given the utilitarian outlook of James Mill and Lord Macaulay, there was very little patience with India's 'irrational' obsessions. In addition, the missionary activity in the nineteenth century set up Hinduism in opposition to Christianity and contributed to the formation of negative opinions. Jyotsna Singh notes, "The eighteenth century Orientalist vision gradually gave way to a new 'discovery' by James Mill in his *History of British India* (1816), in which he defines the ancient Hindu period as the ruin of a decadent civilization, rather than as a pristine Aryan society" (1996:3). Constant comparisons between a monotheistic Christianity and polytheistic Hinduism established the superiority of the former. Add to this the fact that Sanskrit had been dislodged from its position long before the Orientalists lost ground to the Anglicists. The new god of the nineteenth century, the English language, came to serve the civilizing mission. The eighteenth century equation of India as the 'donor' of ancient knowledge had reversed to England becoming the donor of liberalism and science through the English language. In the changed scenario,

Sanskrit was valued neither for intrinsic reasons nor for what it represented. All this formed the kernel of British attitudes towards India in the nineteenth century and contributed to the fading away of Orientalist activities.

The aforementioned translations were carried out by the British as they sought to understand, define and categorize India. Indian intellectuals from the nineteenth century onwards began to intervene and interrupt the colonizer's version of India. Although in many cases terms of argument were informed by the West, the content was from the point of view of the colonized. Indians reacted, responded and redefined and the fulcrum of contestation was once again India's historic past. Given the colonial expropriation of India's past, retrieval of history became an important aspect of the anti-colonial agenda (Panikkar, 1995:112). Translation became a tool to carry out this agenda and issue correction in the Westerner's version of India's past. We see in the nineteenth century various positions articulated vis-à-vis the West through literary exercises (including essays, plays and translations), socio-political tracts and debates. The Bengali elite, especially, had entered into a public dialogue with the colonizer long before English studies were formalized. The advent of printing after 1800 further encouraged Indians looking for self-expression. All this provides us with the context of the first English translation by an Indian – the translation of Sankara's *Vedanta* by the leading reformist, Raja Rammohun Roy.

It is not a coincidence that the significant movement indicated by the reforming and theistic '*samajas*' of modern times was inaugurated by the first Hindu to prepare an English translation of the Upanishads (see Hume, 1934). It is also not a coincidence that Roy was the first Indian intellectual to see the economic and 'cultural' benefits of the English language. His translations were born of his theological predilections and their significance has to be viewed in that context. I believe that their significance in the body of translated literature is historical rather than as influential translations per se. With that in mind, let us look at the intentions governing Roy's decision to translate Indian texts into English and their impact upon his target readers, that is, the Europeans. Rammohun Roy translated first Sankara's *Vedanta* into English, *An Abridgement of the Vedanta* (1816) and then the *Kena* and *Isa Upanishads* (1816) in order to correct "populist misconceptions about India" (Das, 1991:76). By focusing on one particular strand of Hinduism, Roy wanted to establish the fundamental unity of Hinduism and show polytheism to be an encrustation over time. He declares his reasons for translating in the preface:

> In pursuance of my vindication, I have to the best of my abilities translated this hitherto unknown work, as well as abridgment thereof, into the Hindoostanee and Bengalee language, and distributed them, free of cost, among my own countrymen, as widely as circumstances have possibly allowed. The present is an endeavor to render an abridgment of the same into English, by which I expect to prove to my European friends, that the superstitious practices which deform the Hindoo religion have nothing to do with the pure spirit of its dictates. (1816: Introduction)

This attempt to demonstrate that Hinduism has one supreme God was fraught with theological and political implications. Roy's anxiety to purge the ancient sacred tradition of modern-day corruptions glosses over the existence and validity of the multiple identities emerging from Hinduism. This oversimplification is borne out by the complete title of his translation of *Vedanta:* *"Establishing the unity of the Supreme Being; and that He alone is the Object of Propitiation and worship"*. Roy was clearly interpreting Hinduism in the light of Christianity. On the other hand, Roy's determination to 'interpret' Hinduism for the Indians and for the British clearly indicates his choice to translate and historicise the Indian past himself rather than accept 'standard' versions circulated by the British. Ashis Nandy has commented upon the theological cunning underlying Roy's choice of *The Vedas* and *Upanishads* for translations (1983). This matter is debatable and it is not within the scope of this study to discuss it in detail. I do however, wish to point out how the act of translation was invested with the authority of someone who knew both the East and the West and could speak on behalf of both cultures. A reviewer in the Times (2 Oct. 1832) described this first Indian effort as a significant event of the nineteenth century, pointing to Roy's familiarity with both Indian and western literature, and seeing as his main aim exoneration from the charge of idolatry by propounding the unity of one divine Being (see Robertson, 1995:66).

Roy was well versed in the traditions and languages of both the East and the West. This position gave his translations a standing and seriousness made possible for the first time and in the process, rendered the issue of 'fidelity' of the translation, peripheral. Several reviews of Roy's translations recorded in English newspapers show the positive nature of his reception (ibid:1995). Roy represented a new generation of Indian scholars who could intervene in British descriptions of their land. Eminent British Indologists like H.H. Wilson and H.T. Colebrooke quoted him on the subject of *advaita Vedanta*, the only living Indian *'vedantin'* whose authority they acknowledged. Robertson remarks that Wilson presented Roy as a reformer whose translations had sparked off a movement which was breathing new life into a decaying system (ibid:60).

Translations into English by Indians, starting with Roy, were a natural fallout of the Indological translations of the eighteenth century. There were hardly any translations by Indians in the first half of the nineteenth century – very few followed the example of Roy. However, in the late nineteenth century there was a substantial rise in the number. Translations from Sanskrit, which had begun in the eighteenth century by the British, gained momentum in the hands of Indians. These ranged from well-known treatises to poetry and drama. This period produced "dedicated specialists as well as inspired visionaries; and the translation carried out was either philologically accurate to the last detail as in numerous texts on poetics, or was cheerfully liberal as in the renderings by occultists, godmen and social radicals" (Devy, 1993:121). Erudite exercises in translation were aimed at Western Indologists who knew Sanskrit and Indian scholars who knew English. One strand of this phenomenon was translations of works from

Urdu undertaken at Fort William College under the supervision of the principal, the Scotsman John Gilchrist. These were meant to be study materials for the officers of the East India Company. One very popular product of this effort was Mir Amman's *Bagh O Bahar*, translated by Duncan Forbes in 1862.

Towards the end of the century a few contemporary works from Bengali were translated into English. Iswarchandra Vidyasagar's essay on *Marriage of Hindu Widows* in 1856 and *Sermista: A drama in five Acts* were translated by the author Michael Madhusudan Dutt into English in 1859. By and large, Indian translators were for a long time, unable to shed the mantle of the white Indologists and continued to translate only from Sanskrit with a clear focus upon the ancient Hindu past.

An interesting example of translation embedded in the conflicting commitments of its times, is R.C. Dutt's translation of the Indian epics *Ramayana* and *Mahabharata* which, according to the translator, are the "national property" of Indians (Dutt, 1929:155). Dutt had a distinguished career as a member of the Indian Civil Service in British India. He published valuable treatises on the economic history of India and emerged as a crucial figure in India's economic nationalism of the late nineteenth century. His *Lays of Ancient India* included translations of the *Rigveda*, the *Upanishads*, Kalidasa and Bhairavi. Dutt's translations of the Indian epics reflect ideological predilections and highlight the reasons why Indians wanted to translate for a Western audience. Dutt was doing to cultural mythology, what Roy did to religion. If Roy foregrounded the monotheistic elements of Hinduism in order to bring it in line with the religion of the rulers, – Christianity, Dutt's translation of the Indian epics centralized the richness and antiquity of the *Ramayana* and the *Mahabharata* in order to establish their similarity with the two epics of ancient Greece – the *Iliad* and the *Odyssey*. He states, "Ancient India, like ancient Greece, boasts of two great epics. The *Mahabharata*, based on the legends and traditions of a great historical war, is the *Iliad* of India. The *Ramayana*, describing the wanderings and adventures of a prince banished from his country, has so far something in common with the *Odyssey*" (ibid:154). Dutt glorifies the cultural heritage of India and shows how the Hindu epics could be ranked alongside the *Iliad* and the *Odyssey*. It was a common practice at this time to reclaim a glorious past and so to confer dignity upon the present. As Panikkar notes: "The intellectual quest in colonial India, engaged in an enquiry into the meaning of the past and thus in an assessment of its relevance to contemporary society, was an outcome of this awareness" (1995:108). It was important for someone like Dutt, operating within the nationalist paradigm, to invest the present with dignity. Dutt does this by establishing a continuity between the past and the present: "It is not an exaggeration to state that two hundred millions of Hindus of the present day cherish in their hearts the story of their ancient Epics" (1929:154). Dutt also, perhaps not so consciously, resists the essentializing definitions of Hindus prevailing among the British. The commonly held view among most English people, whether liberal Romantics like William Jones or Utilitarians like James Mill, was that the Hindus were by nature indolent and given to submission. In outlining his scheme of translating the two epics, Dutt contests this view by referring to the two different sides of the Hindu: "The *Ramanyana* embodies the domestic and religious life of ancient India, with all its tenderness and sweetness, its endurance and devotion. The *Mahabharata* depicts the political life of ancient India, with all its valour and heroism, ambition and lofty chivalry" (ibid:152). The epics relate to two sides of the Hindus which complement each other. The introductions and epilogues to both epics very clearly address a non-Indian and especially a Western reader. The comparisons with Greek mythology and more importantly Dutt's employment of the Tennysonian Locksley Hall metre are angled towards the reader to whom Indian culture has to be explained in Western terms.

The impact of Dutt's translations could not have been very pervasive among his Indian readers who know him as the author of *The Literature of Bengal* (1879, rev. ed.1895), *A History of Civilization in Ancient India* (3 vols, 1889) and *The Economic History of India* (2 vols, 1902, 1904). M.K. Naik's assessment of the translation is quite unequivocally negative. He says, "While acknowledging fully Dutt's services in making these two great Hindu epics easily accessible to the Western reader in the popular idiom of late Victorianism, the final verdict on his translations must be the same as that well known assessment of Pope's Homer: 'A pretty poem… but not Homer'" (1982:43-44).

The next translation to be considered is that of Dinabandhu Mitra's *Nildurpan*. Nildurpan is a trenchant play, a socio-historical document about indigo planters in Bengal and it appeared first in the Bengali original, in 1860. Within seven months of its publication, *Nildurpan* was translated into English and was sent to England. The copies of the English translation were meant for Europeans who had, according to its publisher expressed a desire to read the play in English (see Gupta, 1972). When the first English edition was brought out, 500 copies were produced for private circulation, of which 202 went to European readers. Not more than 14 copies were circulated in India. Eventually the play was translated into various European and Indian languages and several English editions have appeared since. In a famous trial Rev. James Long was sentenced to imprisonment for publishing *Nildurpan* and almost everyone associated with the English translation of the play was penalized. In the first edition of the original version, the author used a pseudonym – 'A Traveller'. However, Dinabandhu Mitra could not keep his identity secret for long. The reasons for his not disclosing his identity are fairly obvious since the content of the play was very controversial. Through the story of a peasant family and the miseries they undergo at the hands of white indigo planters. The play addresses racial exploitation by the British and belongs to that period after the 1850s, when enthusiasm for British rule was on the wane, a fact manifest in India's first struggle for independence in 1857. Tapan Raychaudhuri reminds us that "the tendency to trace the misfortunes of the rural poor to British arbitrariness and exploitation also go back to this period" (1988:4). Caricatures and satires of English officials became common means of expressing resistance in 'regional' writings of the day. As long as such writings remained in 'regional' languages and the English circle abroad had no access to them through translation, the British government in India did not take the problem seriously.

While Dinabandhu Mitra's play existed in Bengali, it did not interfere with the government. The Bengali version was staged not just before, but even after, a libel suit was instituted against its publisher. The English translation, however, unleashed problems and was fateful in some ways. It appeared seven months after the original play and created a sensation both through its revolutionary content and in the kind of reaction it evoked from the colonial British government. It posed a threat to the government in various ways. The government thought that, if made available to English audiences in England the translation would play havoc with public opinion and the play was promptly banned. Das notes that "the government followed a policy which was not draconian so as to muffle all voices of protest and resistance but was watchful enough to muzzle them whenever it felt threatened" (1995:8). It signaled a drastic change in Indo-British relationships and British attitudes towards what they called 'vernacular' literature and perhaps contributed to some extent towards the making of the Vernacular Act. The identity of the translator of *Nildurpan* remains something of a mystery. The 'invisibility' of the translator here is rather literal. All the English editions state, 'Translated by a Native'. According to the Rev. James Long "both the play and translation are native bonafide productions and depict the Indigo Planting System as viewed by the Natives at large" (Note, *Nildurpan*, 1972). It is widely held that the translator was Michael Madhusudan Dutt, though this has been difficult to establish with certainty.

In a consideration of the trajectory of ILET, the translation of *Nildurpan* is important, but not so much for the controversies surrounding it or any influence upon subsequent translations. Save few exceptional cases of Bankimchandra and Chandu Menon, most works in the eighteenth and nineteenth centuries were from the classical tradition of Sanskrit and Persian. *Nildurpan* in that respect is one of the very few works to be translated from a '*bhasha*' (after G.N. Devy, 1992). If translating the *Vedas* or *Upanishads* or even a literary text was a subscription to the 'great' tradition of Sanskrit, *Nildurpan* was rooted in a more '*desi*' (non-Sanskritic and local) tradition and serves as a counterpoint. Unlike most other translations, *Nildurpan* engages with a burning issue of the day: the indigo plantation. It is perhaps the first translation to be engaged with the immediate and obviously political, and is a change from the glorification of the Indian past in previous translation activity. Finally, the translation of *Nildurpan* and the consequent furore are also a comment upon the censorship and supervision of knowledge transmitted from India to the 'home' country.

At the turn of the century, we find a notable translator translating from various languages – from Latin, Sanskrit, French, Tamil, Gujarati and Bangla into English. Aurobindo was a prolific translator and had definite views on the translation process. He translated parts of the *Ramayana* and the *Mahabharata,* the *Bhagavad Geeta* and selections of Kalidasa from Sanskrit. From Bengali he translated Bankimchandra's *Ananadmath*, but was unable to complete it. He also translated the *Kural* in parts from Tamil. It is difficult to assess the influence of his translations on readers or even to arrive at some sociology of his readership. Such translation exercises were unorganized and sporadic, neither significant nor voluminous enough. While the volume of translations into English continued to be thin for all of the nineteenth and most of the twentieth century, one singular text, *Gitanjali* by Tagore in 1912 became a text of great consequence. In its impact upon the West, *Gitanjali* matches the phenomenon of Jones' *Shakuntalam*. The discussion that follows builds upon the existing industry of commentary on Tagore's translation of *Gitanjali*, its genesis and reception.

Gitanjali

The task of assessing Tagore's translation of *Gitanjali* is both difficult and repetitive. A substantial component of Tagore scholarship in India and abroad is a study of Tagore's translations and in some cases, re-translations of his poetry. Studies of Tagore's *Gitanjali* from a purely textual and now post-colonial point of view attest to Tagore's cavalier and accommodating attitude while translating his own poetry. He received the Nobel Prize for *Gitanjali* and *The Gardener*, but "the constant adjustment to suit the poetics of the colonizer" brought with staggering success quiet embarrassment (Sengupta, 1996:165). The images of a spiritual and mystical East released by Tagore and their divorce from his identity and work in India elicits the following remark:

> There are (at least) two Rabindranath Tagores. One is the most consequential Bengali writer of the century, the author of poems, plays, short stories, songs, memoirs and essays of enduring popularity and importance; the other was a literary sensation in England, America, and Europe in the wake of the publication of *Gitanjali*, a collection of short poems given florid prose translation, in 1912. These two figures have alarmingly little in common, and it is tempting to identify the former as the real Tagore, and the latter as the product of a collectively overheated orientalist imagination... (McDonald, 1997)

Tagore himself was not unaware of the damage he had done to his poetry. He confessed, "When I began this career of falsifying my own coins I did it in play. Now I am becoming frightened of my misdeeds and withdraw into my original vocation as a mere Bengali poet" (1948:264). Sisir Kumar Das notes how Tagore's desire to translate into English was determined by not wanting to remain a 'mere Bengali poet'. However his own effort at translation, was a culmination of well-meaning efforts of personal friends to translate him (see Das, 1994). The turning point took place when Tagore carried his poems to England and W.B. Yeats chanced upon them. The rest, as they say, is history.

The contexts of Tagore's decision to translate and transform his image are marked by some ambiguity. However the response to *Gitanjali* was unequivocal and overwhelming. The book appeared before literary circles at a time when Europe was passing through the very turbulent period preceding the First World War. It also coincided with Tagore's interaction with the West through lectures and talks on religion. This firmly placed the poet-translator as a kind of mystic who had the key to dealing with turmoil and unhappiness. Eminent poets like W.B.Yeats, Ezra Pound and Ernest Rhys welcomed *Gitanjali* as the vision of India from which they were to get a fresher sense of nature and life (see Aronson, 1943:34). The point is that Tagore personified to the West not only his poetry and his message, but also India. The binary dichotomous view that India had spirituality while the West had rationalism was reinforced by the image of Tagore. Tagore was not unaware of the reasons behind the appeal of *Gitanjali*. He tended to lean towards a 'simple' and 'lyrical' kind of poetry when he had to translate into English. *Gitanjali* began to exist in transcendental space, where it had no connection with other sides of Tagore's poetic and political career.

We now turn our attention to an examination of *Gitanjali*'s relationship with other preceding works of translation. The position of *Gitanjali* was different from those of the preceding works in several ways. We have noticed that with translations by Indians so far – whether it was Roy translating the *Upanishads* or Dutt translating the epics – the act of translation was harnessed to the larger goals of revivalism and nationalism. Referring to translations of this period, Kapil Kapoor aptly says that they form part of a "larger process of resistance to the alien domination, an expression of identity, a reassertion of the native self" (1997:153). *Gitanjali* on the other hand was unmistakably authored and its translation rooted in community efforts to project its author to the outside world. *Gitanjali* also marked a new and 'formalist' phase of translation, since translation itself became the primary motive. One can, according to Devy, "consider 1912 as the beginning of translation in India, for it is since then, following Tagore, that Indian translators turned to translating contemporary Indian works" (1993:124). Finally the publication of *Gitanjali* was also the beginning of translation as commercial activity. When Macmillan, London, bought the rights of *Gitanjali* from the India Office, it was with the aim of making it a selling proposition. Several scholars have discussed the escalation of *Gitanjali* in literary and commercial terms and its subsequent 'fall' (see Lago, 1986). The stress here is upon the historical value of *Gitanjali* and its contribution to the body of Indian Literature in English.

There are two things to be said about the impact of the English translation of *Gitanjali* on the Indian subcontinent. For one, it drew an Indian translator's attention to the possibilities of translating into English. The ambition of all Indian writers and translators was undoubtedly fired by the Nobel Prize for Literature in 1913 (see Mukherjee, 1994:10). Soon after *Gitanjali*, Tagore's works were translated extensively into most Indian languages. To give an example, Gujarati registers at least thirty-five different translations of Tagore's works.

However, one also needs to bring to mind that writers like Saratchandra and Bankimchandra from Bengal had travelled to many languages of India without any mediation through English. Translation in India at the beginning of the twentieth century, could not have depended as much on English as it does today. Moreover, Bengali had been a 'donor' language since the eighteenth century and Indian languages had constantly borrowed and translated from Bengali long before *Gitanjali* appeared on the scene. Therefore it is difficult to agree with Das's remark that "the most important role that English played is, undoubtedly, through translation. It is only through a translated text, *Gitanjali*, that Indian literature received international attention and the inter-literary communication within India became easy and quick" (1995:59). There is little doubt, however, of the foundational importance of *Gitanjali* in any systematic consideration of Indian texts in English.

To sum up, the discussion on British translators serves to demonstrate how translation began as an administrative tool and by the time we come to Jones' *Shakuntalam*, it had become a tool with which to 'discover' India. In the hands of the Indian translators, translation acquired a different significance, that of a tool for self-definition and revision of history. *Gitanjali* was a point of departure in this pattern, it inaugurated a modern phase of translation inasmuch as Tagore engaged in it English translation to for personal recognition, not to intervene in the colonial understanding of 'Indian culture'. As a matter of fact, Tagore's project looks back upon a period of spiritual and transcendental texts that characterize the British phase of translation and effectively reinforces Orientalist versions of India. Be that as it may, Tagore's Gitanjali put the Indo-European literary relation on a different scale and footing and serves as the last signpost of English translation in colonial India.

In the meanwhile English translation continued to be a non-institutionalized, sporadic activity till well into the middle of the twentieth century. In the heydays of nationalism and for a few decades after independence, the status of English remained suspect and uncertain. Consequently, literary activities in English for some time remained unattended and English books by Indians unread, as was the case with well-known writers like Raja Rao, Mulk Raj Anand and R.K. Narayan. While the place and relevance of English in India was a question under consideration for some time, the supremacy of the English language as the best 'donor' remained a stable point of view even in post-independence India. Indian languages, nineteenth century onwards, abound in translations from English.

Beginning with the Bible translations by the missionaries at the turn of the centuries to texts like *Aesop's Fables* and *The Pilgrim's Progress*, English translations permeated into the very texture of Indian languages. This phase of English-Indian languages has been the most stable and lasting one and English has also served as a link between European works and India.

As we briefly turn our attention to the nature of intra-Indian translation activity among Indian languages, some patterns emerge. Sisir Kumar Das notes a handful of translations from one Indian language into another in the beginning of the nineteenth century. According to him, these translations were produced to meet the demands of pedagogy and the relationship that first began at the level of textbooks extended to works of knowledge and power (1991:76). Translations from Bengali into other Indian languages were aplenty in the nineteenth century. In addition, Tulsi's *Ramayana* was translated into Urdu, *Bhaktamal* by Nabhaji (a medieval classic in Hindi) was translated into Urdu, the first Marathi novel *Yamuna Paryatan* was translated into Kannada. There are a few more examples, but nothing of a sustained and theorized activity. Some patterns do emerge in early twentieth-century intra-Indian translation activity. As Das (ibid) notes, geographically contiguous literatures had greater scope for translations – for example, Kannada-Marathi and Marathi-Gujarati. Similarly, the cluster of Dravidian languages have had greater interaction among each other than with languages of the North. Perceptions of 'richness' in a specific literature maintained by members of other linguistic communities also governed the course of translation. Bengali, in that respect, has through translation enjoyed the greatest prestige.

Shifts can be discerned even in terms of the actual act of translation. The episode of English translation in India introduced the preoccupations of a Western translator into the Indian tradition. It was mentioned earlier that in pre-colonial India, translations took place largely from Sanskrit into other Indian languages. While these continued unabated, they illustrated a shift from a 'liberal' attitude mentioned earlier to a more scholarly approach. For instance, the well-known reformist and Gujarati writer Navalram recommends an attitude of an "obedient servant" in his review of a translation from Sanskrit into Gujarati (1966:52-53). On the other hand, in his own translation of Moliere's *Mock Doctor* into Gujarati, he identifies three types of translation (*'Shabdanusar'*: word to word, *'Arthanusar'*: sense to sense; and *'Rasanusar'*: spirit to spirit) in a Dryden-like manner (ibid:16-17). He advises translators to choose the third kind of translation and re-contextualise a foreign work of art to suit the native poetics (ibid). It is interesting that Indian translators' 'professional' attitude towards Sanskrit did not extend to European works. There are in many Indian languages vigorous traditions of European works in free translation as well as deftly done adaptations. The 'Indianization' of Shakespeare in Indian languages is one such story. The cultural and political implications of these exercises constitute a fresh area of investigation, but it is beyond the scope of my study.

The institutionalization of translation took place in independent India in 1947. As a sovereign nation-state, India felt the need to invent, foreground and bestow common symbols upon a conglomerate of different linguistic states. The State perceived the need to establish common links among different linguistic communities and create literary awareness of all literatures. Issues of translation in post-independence India are intricately connected with the new identities that emerged in the light of the bifurcation of the Indian landscape along linguistic lines. Issues of language and nation acquired new emphases and have since then in/directly determined the course of translation activity in India.

3.   The Two-Worlds Theory

"Language. Everywhere Krishna went as a journalist, she found she carried it with her like a caste mark. It was at once her identity and her sorrow."

Krishna, the chief protagonist from Mrinal Pande's *My Own Witness* (2000:156) records her experiences as a Hindi newspaper journalist, marked and marginalized, in the English-dominated media world of post-independence India.

It is only too true that language shapes identity, especially in India. One of the first and perhaps the most divisive battles fought in post-independence India was over language (Memon and Banerji, 1997:98). Language became a way of providing a base, a ground for laying down roots. This by itself is not new to any culture – languages have always been strong markers of identity. What is significant however, is the strong conflation between what may be called 'mother-tongue' and identity that became evident in the wake of Indian independence. Before we come to discuss the changes in India's linguistic economy in post- independence India, it is useful to underscore the inextricable link between language and translation. It goes without saying that translation is not merely a linguistic activity. At the same time, perceptions of and relationships with specific languages give rise to translation. The following discussion throws light on a reconfigured relationship in post-independence India between (some) Indian languages and the English language, determining the context for a necessary bilingualism and biculturalism. While the previous chapter showed a preponderance of Sanskrit and to a certain extent, Persian, as SLs for English, the present one indicates a marked shift in the story of English translation. The movement away from classical languages towards more homespun 'mother-tongues' in post-independence India is manifest in translation, among other things. It implies the renewed roles that both mother tongues as well as English have come to play albeit the relationship between the two does not admit of complete ease even today. At the same time, the English translation activity points to beginnings of a more dialogic, mutually profitable relationship in future.

Given the tremendous complexity of India's linguistic situation, a broad classification of languages in India would serve well for a beginning. About 400-odd languages are spoken in India, although the Census of India documents not more than 114. Of these 114, the Eighth Schedule of the Indian Constitution extends official recognition to only 18 scheduled languages into English. Of these 18 languages, some correspond to geographical boundaries and enjoy distinct advantages in 'linguistic states' and are very often referred to as 'regional languages'. Languages that do not correspond to geographical boundaries may still be considered 'regional' languages, but they lack the infrastructure in terms of schools and printing and publishing presses. The regional languages operating in the linguistic states of India and scheduled in the Indian Constitution form one power-cluster. Languages brushed aside as minor or as dialects by the state remain outside this cluster and form another, and in fact, bigger, group.

Again, this group consists of oral as well as written languages. Also, within the roster of officially recognized languages, not all of them enjoy equal prestige. Thus, the linguistic map of India is rife with inequalities, a condition not helped much by the English language. This chapter is concerned not so much with the peculiar dynamics operating among Indian languages, as with their steady growth in post-independence India and the relationships they come to form with English. The first half of the discussion below points to two parallel developments in post-independence India – stronger interlocking between language and identity, reinforced by the linguistic re-organization of states and the increasing role played by the English language. The latter half examines how these two developments have created conditions for bilingualism ('regional language' and English), and also reset the terms between what was earlier derogatively referred to as the 'vernacular' and English, specially for the well-heeled middle class of India. It is in this context that we shall situate the activity of English translation.

Mother Tongue

In 1947, India, determined to organize itself as a sovereign nation-state, found itself faced with a mass of different languages, different styles, customs and food, rendering Indianness a nebulous and fuzzy construct. The nation needed centralizing imperatives as well as a federal arrangement for democratic functioning. The former required a 'national' language, while the latter required the legitimizing of more specific identities. The issue of the national language, as we shall see later, became very tricky and never acquired a common consensus. However, the bifurcation of states along linguistic lines gave (some) regional languages their specific legitimacy and space. Sunil Khilnani (1997) considers this as the state's attempt at creating a 'layered' identity of a region and a nation, although, as we shall see later, the intention to bifurcate on the basis of language was not entirely sociocultural.

After about fifty years of India's formation as a republic, it is becoming apparent that ethnic identities have been greatly moulded by linguistic identities in India. Some of the processes strengthening this go back to the 1950s. It is not being implied here that there was no regional consciousness in India before the sovereign state. Indians have traditionally perceived themselves as Oriyas or Gujaratis – an all-pervasive regional identity has always been the strongest. However, the sharpening of 'regional consciousness' that manifested itself through an affiliation with the 'mother tongue' was one of the reactions to colonialism. The perception that the 'mother tongue' served best as the community conduit had taken hold of a Bankimchandra in the nineteenth century, and a Gandhi in the twentieth. The orientalists faded out of the controversy over knowledge and cultural production fairly early on, and the dispute was then carried on mainly between the anglicists and the 'regionalists' or 'vernacularists'. This was because knowledge and cultural production were no longer seen as resting with the 'oriental' languages, but with the 'regional' languages (Mukherjee, M. 2000).

English officials involved in the framing of English studies were not unaware of the reach 'rude' and 'barbaric' dialects such as Marathi and Bangla had in specific regions. *Woods's Despatch* shows regular translation of English textbooks into regional languages, and then their prescription for general education (see Aggarwal, 1993, 2nd ed.). After all it was in these languages that the "entire project of English in India is internalized, and also occasionally assessed and critiqued" (Mukherjee, M. 2000:3). Thus, the process of disseminating information and knowledge through 'regional languages' was well under way after the nineteenth century. A positive evaluation of the 'mother-tongues' had begun, in recognition of their efficacy for the masses. Given the fact that this process had been set in motion since the nineteenth century, the reorganization of the linguistic states did not come as a surprise. The aim of creating linguistic states as manageable, governing units was an administrative one. The nation-state needed a democracy that could function on a consensus of regional units and the strength of the 'Centre'. B.R. Ambedkar saw the division of states along the linguistic lines as a democratic inevitability. He stated:

> A linguistic province produces what democracy needs, namely, social homogeneity and makes democracy work better than it would in a mixed province. There is no danger in creating linguistic provinces with the language. (1992:649)

As an outcome of consolidating specific linguistic groups, the Bombay Province was bifurcated into the states of Gujarat and Maharashtra in 1960. Punjab and Haryana came to be divided in 1966. In the early 70s the Northeast was reorganized into new states and Union Territories. The formation of Andhra Pradesh as a new linguistic state left a trail of very unhappy incidents. On the whole, language issues had become dangerously prickly in India, "touching the chords of the growing regionalism which was engulfing India, but also at pride and intensity" (Memon and Banerji, 1997:100).

For the languages that did form a majority, as defined by the Eighth Schedule of the Indian Constitution, this majority could be translated into a space, a territory, and an infrastructure. The infrastructure networks of education and publishing activities gave impetus to the fourteen languages that corresponded with fourteen states. The scope and tendency of the language of the majority to expand through the institutionalization processes of the linguistic state (although this does not apply to all languages), increased. In the process of studying the historic expansion of Indian-language newspapers in India, Robin Jeffrey notes that the circulation of daily newspapers in all languages trebled between 1976 and 1992 – from 9.3 million to 28.1 million and the dailies-per-thousand people ratio doubled – from 15 daily newspapers per 1000 people to 32 per 1000 (1993:2004-2010). Infrastructure supported by a regional state apparatus may have contributed to the growth of literary-cultural productions so visible after the 1960s. In fact Jeffrey's study is limited to the 'majority languages' of the linguistic states, and he notes that one of the reasons why Urdu newspapers do not show these tendencies is because Urdu is not the language of education (1997:631-635). The point to be emphasized here is that the linguistic state may have, by providing infrastructure, contributed further to the growth of the 'regional languages', and by extension, 'regional literatures'. However, as mentioned earlier, tensions between one 'regional language' and another within the same state or between states still continue to take place. The controversy about Urdu, the riots in the wake of the 'imposition' of Hindi, the divided opinions about English, the quarrels between Oriya and Bengali, or Marathi and Konkani – are but a few illustrations that serve to demonstrate how "language forms and ruptures social identities" in India (Kaviraj, 1992:25). At the same time, the role of the linguistic state, at least for its 'main' language cannot be underscored. The distinct rise in the confidence and quantity of cultural productions, as well as the strengthening of regional identity through education and culture may be considered connected with India's federal arrangement on the basis of language.

It can be concluded from the foregoing that factors related to the nineteenth century such as the contact with English literature, the advent of printing, and the formation of the linguistic state, have all contributed to the expansion of regional languages, and the effects are visible in the sheer quantity and vibrancy of regional literatures. In the meanwhile, post-independence India has also witnessed a mind-boggling expansion in the English language. Despite being a colonial relic and a neo-colonial instrument, English also functions today as an Indian language and fits into India's linguistic universe without causing too much heartburn. Rushdie notes that the children of independent India seem not to think of English as being irredeemably tainted by its colonial provenance (discussed in Prasad, 1999). The discussion below traces the journey that English has travelled to arrive at its present stage of acceptance and competence, largely in the Indian middle class, and more specifically, in the younger generations of the middle and upper-middle classes in India.

Other Tongue

India's official policy regarding English was riddled with contradictions and brought in its wake very strong opinions for and against the retention of English. In any case, Nehruvian policies regarding language, economics and commerce in the years following Independence firmly established the importance of English. English has remained central to public discourses in India and this centrality is reinforced today by the advances in Information and Technology.

In 1947, the newly independent nation-state recognized the importance of English, and it was legally sanctioned by the Constitution as the associate official language. The retention of this colonial legacy in the postcolonial nation-state did not come as a surprise to many. English had come to perform several functions in India after 1900. Ahmad notes that the national intelligentsia was rooted in English education and used English for several purposes in colonial India (1994:76). The new middle class formed in the nineteenth century was partly a product of education in English. This does not mean that the use of English was entirely free of cultural confrontation. However, when the country became politically free there were already huge networks of education and bureaucracy resting on the foundation of English (see Burde and Krishnaswamy, 1998). In addition, India's decision, or rather the decision of the Nehruvian government, to take the path of industry and commerce rather than follow the pre-independence agrarian economy, increased the importance of English. Nehru's government recognized the importance of English as the language of the future. While the anti-English nationalists denounced English because it represented a humiliating past, the supporters of English saw it as signalling an elevated future. The position of English vacillated between these two points of view. Opinions for and against English were strong on both sides. At the same time, emotionally and politically, it was clear that English could not become the 'national' language. Hindi was named the official language and the decision created no small degree of mayhem. The Southern States perceived Hindi as a language of the North and hence a symbol of the North's colonization of the South (Memon and Banerji, 1997:99). English carried hazy memories of colonialism, eclipsed by aspirations and economic gifts, not only for the South, but also for the middle class of India. On the other hand, Hindi was a symbol of hegemony for some, but without any promise of progress. Vested interests on both sides have since then kept the 'national' language in abeyance and consequently, Hindi and English continue to be bound together in an unhappy and mutually undermining partnership. English and Hindi came to stand for the two camps of the 'colonial-minded' elite and the 'nationalists' respectively. The battle over English made its position in India very uncertain.

In a move that temporarily circumvented the issue, the Constitution projected the gradual replacement of English as an instrument of the state within 15 years after 1950. The arbitrary and half-hearted nature of this decision is captured by R.K. Narayan with characteristic irony in his story *Fifteen Years*. Here is an excerpt of a conversation between the English language and a judge who wants to oust English (1998:20):

English: You probably picture me as a trident-bearing Rule Britannia, but actually I am a devotee of Goddess Sarasvati. I have been her most steadfast handmaid.

Judge: All that is beside the point. Even if you come in a sari with kumkum on your forehead we are going to see that you are deported. The utmost we shall allow you will be another fifteen years...

'Fifteen years from what time?' Asked the English language, at which the judge felt so confused that he ordered, 'I will not allow any more discussion on this subject', and rose for the day.

The Constitution continued to make guarantees for the extension of English and the fifteen-year limit became a mythical concept. A report of the Official Language Commission in 1956 recommended the use of English for law-courts and in the administration of justice. The Official Language Act (OLA) of 1963 allowed its use for all Union purposes. Finally, in 1967, with the amendment to the OLA, English acquired a special status in the Constitution as an "associate official language" of the Union without any time limit. One of the ways out of the Hindi-English bind along with the claims of other regional languages was the much-touted three-language formula. According to this, three languages – the regional, the national (Hindi), and the international (English) should be studied by every Indian school-going child. The programme was devised with a view to privileging the regional language within a given state, teaching Hindi for national and inter-regional communication and English for progress and scientific thought. For several reasons, this remained a desired goal rather than a reality.

The post-independence fervour for one language as the focus of national unity began to ebb away. As things stand now, Government propaganda expresses support and encouragement for Hindi, but social and economic opportunities favour English. The Judiciary, the Education Department, the print and visual media and all bodies of the Central government support English. English is the language of a very small urban minority that does not amount to more than 3 per cent in a population of one billion. This anomaly is difficult to comprehend unless we take account of the fact that this 'minority' in a densely populated country adds up to 25 to 30 million speakers. The urban and English-knowing elite of India appears small in relative terms, but matches the population of both Australia and New Zealand. This so-called minuscule fraction of the population is spread mainly in the metropolitan centres and is firmly entrenched in powerful positions.

It should be noted here that Hindi is the most widely spoken language of India, but English is guarded by ideological, regional and class interests (see Rajan, 1992). As a result, supporters of Hindi appear a doggedly unrealistic lot. As far as the administration is concerned, the use of Hindi has become "… ceremonial rather than communicative. The dissemination of Hindi over the years has occurred, perhaps not through government fiat, but with the help of the Hindi visual media" (Krishna, 1991:66). Hindi cinema in particular serves as a defining image of India and is one of its most prolific cultural industries. Hindi cinema has contributed tremendously to the spoken forms of Hindi, keeping up some minimum levels of competence in the Central and Northern states of India. However, as the language of higher education and economic opportunities, English is the most sought after language of India. In some senses, English merely succeeds Sanskrit, Persian and Urdu as a language of prestige, articulating power and privilege at different points in sub-continental history. Yet the authority represented by English today has in many ways superseded the Sanskrit heritage of the *'pandits'*, not to mention the Persian lingua franca of the Moghuls. Sanskrit has been an exalted language of the scriptures, but never a spoken language in India. Persian too was essentially a language of administration. English on the other hand, is emerging as a widely used spoken and written language for the urban elite in India, and as a language of wider communication even internationally for a certain class. There is a fair amount of debate regarding the class that patronizes the English language and takes a minimum level of English for granted. By and large, both the elite and the middle class of India living in its metropolitan cities seem to emerge as the chief mainstay of the English language. The fragmentation and amorphous nature of the English speaking class defies any coherent classification. In Pavan Varma's opinion, it burgeoned through English education and colonial administration in the nineteenth century and is today the rampantly consumerist and apolitical section of the society (1998). Gurcharan Das, on the other hand, prefers to distinguish between the old bourgeoisie of the nineteenth and twentieth century and a new "consuming class" formed in the last decades of the millenium (2000). What emerges as an undeniable fact and the one that interests us here is that in India this class is largely formed by city-dwelling, English-fluent people (hereafter, for convenience, 'middle class') who in the absence of a 'national' language, employ English as a link language. An equally undeniable feature of any argument about the middle class is its power in shaping and moulding policies, markets and culture. After the economic reforms of 1991 that released India from the old 'License Raj' and allowed a global play of market forces, this middle class has become the chief market for the multinationals. Formed through processes of urbanization and education, this class supports English the most. Given its huge presence and the power it has over networks of education, the judiciary and the media, English proliferates with the expansion of the middle class. Gurcharan Das remarks:

> … whether old or new, the middle class is growing very rapidly in India. If one draws a line from Kanpur to Madras, I reckon that by 2020, half the population west of the line will be middle class. It will take about twenty years for half the people east of the line to get there. By then, 650 million Indians will be middle class, and this will have a major impact on politics, markets, and society. (ibid:319)

From detergent soaps to satellite television, the economic base consuming these products has grown wider and wider in the last decade and a half. Varma notes that the satellite revolution commenced in 1991. By 1995, it was estimated that more than eighteen million homes were wired to cable or satellite (1998:178). In these economic and cultural interactions that the middle class effects with globalization, English acquires a central place in reinforcing the global links.

We call once again to mind that in post-independence India we see (1) a strengthening of regional literary and linguistic traditions and (2) the rise of English as an Indian language. These twin phenomena are mirrored in the expansion of bilingual processes involving English and a 'regional' language, as testified by a recent study of the significant rise of English as a second language. Vijayunni notes that out of the 80.7 core population speaking the scheduled languages, nine core Indians know English as a second or third language (11.15 per cent of the population), while the corresponding figure for Hindi is seven core (*The Hindu*, 16th July, 1999).

In fact, patterns of traditional Indian multilingualism (whereby Indians knew more than at least two to three other Indian languages) are reduced to a bilingualism involving English and the various 'regional languages' (see Kaviraj, 1992; Ahmad, 1994). Also, if bilingualism amounts to an equal proficiency in both languages, we need to use the term somewhat tentatively. What we witness today is an undeniable frequent and comfortable slipping and sliding from an Indian language into English and vice-versa. The nature of the interaction between an Indian language and English includes everyday speech as well as literary and media scripts that reflect such 'bilingual' processes. Advertisement captions, news reports and articles, Indian writing in English and ILET are only some manifestations of a profoundly contemporary Indian ethos that shows today a greater simultaneity of Indian language and English. While linguists may prefer to call this 'code-switching', it is not merely a syntactical or a lexical event. It speaks of an urban and educated Indian's sense of comfort in accommodating the two worlds represented by the two languages. In fact, this moment of bilingualism is a peculiarly postcolonial moment in which both English and an Indian language sit comfortably next to each other. The cultural identity formed by English added to a layer of a 'mother-tongue' is the stuff of a contemporary urban middle class.

Sugata Srinivasraju aptly describes this bilingualism as a "cleverly engineered cultural idea has come to support pragmatically the very idea of India" (2001:62). It is important to note that the terms of this relationship are far from equal, – after all, the 'mother-tongue' represents for the urban Indian a 'regional', therefore limited, world. English, on the other hand, is the cosmopolitan language.

This regional-cosmopolitan nexus may be seen as the Indian middle class response to the worldwide use of English and its own need to maintain a linguistic identity. The arrangement sounds more amicable than it actually is – English has the upper hand in the bargain. By rendering the 'regional language' as less relevant for economic reasons, English draws most of the intellectual energy towards itself. However, some of this threatening edge is lost when it is also used to further the cause of a 'regional language'.

This explains a (wistful?) longing among Indian intellectuals for its own regional literatures which suffer from apparent marginalization. This is also coupled with the feeling the so-called marginalization of regional literatures has both its root and solution in the English language. English translation needs to be viewed in this context. English is emerging, willy-nilly, as the only choice for expressing and promoting 'regional' languages and culture. The nature of this process as neo-colonial, subversive, or postcolonial may be a subject of heated debate. Are regional languages now 'employing' English on their own terms and making it serve as a conduit? Or is English, as Trivedi (1996) suggests, effecting a cultural totalitarianism and as usual, calling the shots? The interaction is fairly complex and dialogic and we must examine the specific case of English translation in India.

Traditionally, and as discussed in an earlier chapter, translations flow from an elite, donor language into presumably inferior, receptor languages. The instances of Sanskrit into the bhashas and Latin into English are too well known to repeat here. English, after the nineteenth century acquired a similar status of a 'donor' language and Indian regional languages received much from English to enrich their 'crude' state of existence! We see this trend and equation between Indian languages and the English language as continuing from the 19th century till almost the middle decades of the twentieth century. Strikingly, in the years after the 1980s, there appeared to be a seeming reversal in this equation. However, in fact, the terms of the relationship are far from being reversed.

Undoubtedly, English is emerging as the most accepted and 'natural' receptor for literatures produced in the 'regional languages', but given its dominance the world over, it does not carry the usual connotations of a 'receptor' language. At one level, therefore, English continues to be unchanged in its role of a dominating language and nothing has altered that position. At a different level, however, English itself is being internalized, appropriated and made use of in the process of 'carrying' the 'regional' ethos. Thus, the situation is neither one of 'confrontational neutrality', nor of an unequivocal totalitarianism. A celebratory approach towards English translation that privileges the 'binding' role played by the English language in a multilingual country masks the cultural and political implications of this interaction. On the other hand, to see English only as an icon of cultural and political hegemony is to lose sight of the fact that English has also emerged as a response to some profound sociological needs of the Indian middle class. English translation, by being an interface between the Indian language on one hand and English on the other, carries the story of English's reconfigured relationship with Indian languages today. As an illustration of this phenomenon, and also as one more signpost in the history of English translation, we now turn to the case of A.K. Ramanujan.

A. K. Ramanujan

Ramanujan, unlike his predecessors who translated into English, translated to draw attention to non-classical and non-elite discourses. English, in his scheme of things, came to play a new role – that of foregrounding stories, tales, legends and literatures from the 'kitchen' languages. Fully sentient to the linguistic pluralism as well the linguistic violence in India, Ramanujan wanted to emphasize 'little' traditions through translations. His translations of the Virasaiva poets (*Speaking of Shiva,* 1973), or the folk tales (*Folktales from India: A Selection of Oral Tales from Twenty-two Languages,* 1991) and the love poems (*The Interior Landscape: Love Poems from a Classical Tamil Anthology*, 1967) illustrate this very well. As an English teacher as well as an Indian English poet, Ramanujan was aware of the inevitability of English in disseminating an alternative view of the Indian society. Hence, he brought to the forefront not only his expertise and equal comfort in working with Kannada and English, as well as Tamil and English, but also opened up possibilities of bringing Kannada and Tamil to centre stage. After the 1960s, Ramanujan had become one of the most influential post-Orientalist and anti-colonial voices in South Asian and comparative inter-disciplinary studies: he opposed the historically and culturally homogenizing 'Sanskritist' vision of India that was still hegemonic among European and Anglo-American area-specialists in the Cold War decades, and emphasized the immense linguistic, regional, and diachronic diversity of the subcontinent's cultures (V. Dharwadker, 1994). Ramanujan was operating from the context of anthropology and linguistics, where the awareness of what constitutes 'high' and 'low', 'great' and 'little' traditions is quite sharp. His forays into disciplines such as linguistics, anthropology and ethnography and his own standing as a modernist poet in English, form a backdrop. As a linguist, Ramanujan was interested in the non-classical, *'desi'* languages, as opposed to classical languages such as Persian and Sanskrit. He called the former "kitchen-languages/mother-tongues" and the latter "market-languages/father-tongues" (ibid). According to Ramanujan, cultural memories and truths lay in the kitchen-languages rather than the more dominating father-tongues. This view was in tandem with Milton Singer's well-known division of 'great' and 'little' traditions. Classical traditions exist and continue, very often, at the cost of smaller homegrown traditions. (Incidentally, Ramanujan was teaching in Chicago, the breeding ground of Singer's ideas). All this led Ramanujan to believe that Sanskrit had been over-emphasized in India, while other Indian languages, especially ancient Tamil and Kannada, had been marginalized. "Through his translations from Tamil and Kannada into English, Ramanujan was trying to restore this balance", suggests Harish Trivedi (personal interview). For us, it is relevant to note that Ramanujan was 'employing' English to issue some historical correction about languages and their hitherto shadowy existence in India. This consciousness informs much of the English translation activity, a subject we continue to be concerned with in the following chapter. In the meanwhile, it is crucial to keep in mind that merely asserting the importance of translation as a binding force in India's multilingualism does not uncover its embeddedness in socio-political dynamics within Indian languages as well English. Also, when we talk of regional languages in English translation, it is crucial to ask, as Rukmini Bhaya Nair does, "So is the adjective 'regional' to be equated with the idea that it emanates from a political entity known as the 'linguistic state'?" She remarks: "Blithely providing 'quality' translation without an accompanying debate on matters of regionalism, and linguistic power is to neglect to build foundations for the important project of literary translation" (1998:77).

4. Within Academia

The central question that this chapter is concerned with is, "Why translation now?" The thematic trajectory of English translation in India provided in the first chapter established Tagore's *Gitanjali* (1913) as a landmark heralding literary translation as an exercise for wider dissemination. Tagore's enterprise of translation was not altogether free of the anxieties of a colonial subject. However, unlike the English translations of the previous century, it was neither 'nationalistic' nor 'reformistic' in an obvious way. The impact of *Gitanjali* notwithstanding, translation from Indian languages into English remained an uninstitutionalized, sporadic activity till well into the middle of the twentieth century. The nation-state institutionalized translation and creative writing for the first time through the National Book Trust (1957) and the Sahitya Akademi (1954). Literature, along with music, dance and theatre seemed one of the ways to bring different communities together. The push towards creating pan-Indian forms and reinforcing 'unity-in-diversity' fitted well with the Nehruvian vision of India. Keeping that in mind, semi-government institutions like the Sahitya Akademi chose to confer awards on 'reputed' works from each language and undertook to translate them from one Indian language into another. English hardly ever figured in this scheme of 'nation-building.' As discussed earlier, the fate of English remained uncertain, in official terms, till the sixties.

Sixties onwards, we witness an increase in English publishing activities by Indians, a matter discussed in some detail subsequently. English translations from Indian languages acquired a tiny slot with some publishers such as Jaico, Vikas and Asia. Around the same time, UNESCO's collection of Representative Works chose Indian works for translation into other languages of the world, including English. In addition to this, P. Lal, the Indian English poet and translator founded the Writer's Workshop in 1958. This one-man publishing house published literature written and 'transcreated' (a term coined by P. Lal for readable and not strictly faithful translation) into English and thereby provided a much-needed forum to many poets and translators of English. A.K. Ramanujan was one among the many poets and translators that P. Lal published. We have discussed Ramanujan's unique place in the history of English translation earlier. At this point, it is useful to mention that Ramanujan also introduced a 'modern' and acceptable idiom for English translations. His use of unsentimental and terse idiom (derived partly from the kinds of texts he worked with and partly his own modernist leanings) served as a model for future translators. Today Ramanujan's translations have come under severe attack by Tejaswini Niranjana (1992), but that does not undermine the exemplary nature of his work. In a translation career spanning almost three decades, Ramanujan made English translations appear sophisticated and professional for the first time. With all this, however, Ramanujan remained a solitary example of a 'successful' translator for years. Harish Trivedi offers an apt evaluation by stating, "Ramanujan was doing a one-man job. He was not a part of any movement in India, but he was definitely a precursor" (personal interview, 1998).

In the meanwhile, translation activity continued to limp for a host of reasons. There seemed a dearth of good translators and readership, and more importantly, the universal and narrow perception of translation as inferior and secondary continued to assail the motivation behind translation. This limitation seemed particularly acute in the case of English because it was seen as an inadequate TL for carrying across the 'regional' ethos. Be that as it may, sporadic efforts continued which must be mentioned. For instance, in the seventies, the Oxford University Press brought out a set of Indian plays in English translation through its imprint named 'Three Crowns'. While the importance of these occasional gestures cannot be downplayed, the lack of continuity and consistency was undeniable. Prabhakar Machwe, secretary of the Sahitya Akademi in the seventies complained that "even after 25 years, we have not been able to develop a team of ten good, competent translators of Indian languages into English"(1979: 141).

Since the late eighties, there have been dramatic changes in the production, reception and respectability of literary translations into English. This is not an a-historical phenomenon that has taken place in a vacuum; it has grown out of a range of disciplinary and socio-cultural contexts that feed into and source it. Some of these contexts are unique to India, while a few others partake of global developments at large. Similarly, English translation is also informed by the legacies outlined in the first chapter and the changes in the linguistic economy of India discussed in the second chapter. With all this in mind, we now turn our attention to the range of determinants that provide an academic and cultural sanction to this activity. Academic and extra-academic determinants intersect to make literary productions acceptable at institutional and social levels. It is difficult and undesirable to separate the two, but in order to keep the focus restricted, the following discussion delineates the academic component of this consensus.

It is not a matter of coincidence that departments of English in many Indian universities have begun to offer courses on translation and/or Indian literature in English in the last fifteen years. For instance, South Gujarat University (Surat); North Gujarat University (Patan); Saurashtra University (Rajkot) and Gujarat University offer courses on Translation Theory and Practice at the M.Phil/Ph.D levels. Students translate a work of art in lieu of a dissertation and thereby add to the body of unpublished works in translation. Some universities, such as Gujarat University and University of Madras offer a paper on ILET that allows the consumption of texts in translation. The Comparative Literature programme of Jadavpur University (JU), has been offering a section on 'Translation Studies' in its MA programme beginning with the batch that took MA finals in 1996. The developments in the Gujarat and Madras Universities also belong to the nineties. Delhi University began to offer an M. Phil in Literature and Translation in the late eighties (the course is now split into Comparative Literature and Translation.). Bangalore University began offering a course on translation at the MA and M. Phil levels as early as 1981. Himachal University offers a paper on translation theory as well Indian literature in English translation. The University of Hyderabad has been at the vanguard of Translation Studies for the last fifteen years. In some cases, the English departments extended recognition to courses on Indian literature in English translation much before it became an academic trend. For instance, Jadavpur University began to offer the course from the mid-seventies and Bangalore University since 1981. The inclusion of literary translation as theory or as texts contributes to both production as well as reception. The two processes of production and consumption are intertwined and it is sometimes difficult to know what follows what. The establishment of systematic publishing programmes for translation also coincides with the changes in the curriculum. In the meanwhile, after the eighties, review journals such as the *Indian Review of Books*, *The Book Review* and *Biblio* also began to circulate with regularity among the English-reading public of urban India and provided news of books written and translated into English. It is now common to see special numbers of these journals, time and again, devoted to the subject of translation. The newly instituted prizes and awards for translation have already been mentioned in the opening chapter. All these are signs of our times and point to the fact that Indian texts in English translation are gaining ground at several levels.

Undeniably, the growth of ILET is less dramatic than that of the Indian English novel. Translations into English also show a preponderance of fiction, but Indian novels in English translation do not draw as much attention and notice as those written in English. The international profile of the Indian English novel has made it an eye-catching phenomenon, that has not gone unnoticed even by general readers. On the other hand, notes Meenakshi Mukherjee that "another phenomenon that is also acquiring a boom-status within the country ... translation of Indian fiction in English" (1998:34) is little talked about. How the two literary phenomena compare with each other and the dynamics they share forms an area of investigation in the next essay. My purpose here is to historicize this less glamorous, but steadily increasing body, and it seems appropriate to begin with the way the theoretical perception of translation has changed over the years.

Translation Theories: Here and There

Translation is one of the major ways in which literatures enter into contact and interfere with each other and yet few literary histories anywhere in the world ever acknowledge this fact. India is no exception. Cultural exchanges between the major and minor (now called '*marga*' and '*desi*', after G.N. Devy, 1992) streams have taken place largely through translation. In that sense, India has, in Devy's phrase, a "translating consciousness" (see Devy, 1998a). A continuous straddling of different languages by its multilingual citizens has made translation in India a familiar and everyday affair, hardly worth theorizing. Very little thought has been expended by Indian scholars on the aesthetics of translation or the place of translated texts in literary systems. This lack of theorization has hindered neither the everyday nature of translation nor the unplanned literary exchanges between one Indian language and another. English translation has also borne the consequences of this general indifference towards a systematic consideration. In addition, and perhaps more importantly, it has suffered from the limitations posed by the English language in conveying an indigenous ethos. This cardinal limitation of the language is still not done away with, but possibilities of circumventing it have now opened up. Eighties onwards, scholars of translation invited and challenged Indian translators into English and articulated theoretical issues regarding the activity. Sujit Mukherjee made a pioneering gesture through *Translation as Discovery* ((1980) 1991). Mukherjee voiced his reservations about English translation activity as a less satisfactory activity compared with translations from one Indian language into another. At the same he admitted the increasing importance of what he referred to as "Indo-English" (now, ILET) as one that may contribute to forming a 'link' literature for India. Mukherjee's book undoubtedly served as the first-ever-systematic account of English translation activity in India. By the time Mukherjee's book went into a second reprint in 1992, the act as well as the activity of English translation had received considerable fillip. G.N. Devy's collection of essays titled *In Another Tongue* (1993) and *Of Many Heroes: Essays in Indian Historiography* (1998a) included, among other things, essays on translation. Devy asserted the importance of translating into English but expressed a need to evolve Indian approaches to translation. Devy critiqued what he perceived as the West's paranoia of translation manifest in anxieties regarding the faithfulness of the text. Tejaswini Niranjana's *Siting Translation* (1992) marked a further advance in translation studies. Niranjana drew attention to the collusion between English translation and the agenda of imperialism in creating a textualised version of India. She stressed upon the postcolonial, resistant subject's need to "re-translate" and thereby "re-write history". In an equally critical vein, Aijaz Ahmad through his *In Theory* (1994) drew attention to the 'archive' of literary translations in English through which the so-called Third World Literature enters the western academy for selection and consumption. The instances of translated texts entering into the West's academic-literary marketplace are few, and as such, Ahmad's comment is valid in terms of a possibility, rather than an historical event. Ahmad echoes Sujit Mukherjee when he comments, "Meanwhile, it is in English more than any other language that the largest archive of translation has been assembled so far; if present trends continue, English will become, in effect, the language in which the knowledge of 'Indian' literature is produced" (ibid:250). Opinions on whether English translation is a satisfactory activity or not, continue to be divided among Indian academics, albeit a tacit recognition of its inevitability. Eminent critics and translators such as Meenakshi Mukherjee (1998) and Harish Trivedi (1996) have voiced their disapproval of the undue attention paid to English (as opposed to intra-Indian) translation. Such interventions contribute to the process of 'thinking about translation,' and keep interest in the field sustained. Out of these academic notes on translation, no homogeneous or even systematic translation theory has emerged. The common backdrop, however, of the eighties and the nineties runs through them. Before we arrive at any link (or lack thereof) between these theoretical formulations and the production of texts in India, let us turn to translation theories in the West.

Academic investment in issues of translation in India have been spurred on by and have contributed to translation theories in the West. The criss-crossing of global and local productions, especially of the intellectual kind, involves very complex negotiations. It is difficult to ascertain the extent to which translation theories may have had an impact on the production of texts, and yet a nexus between academic and market shifts is undeniable. Radical shifts in the disciplines of Translation Studies and Departments of English may indicate possibilities of creating new canons which may, in turn, absorb texts. The perception of translation as a discursive, complex, political activity has had far-reaching effects on the institutionalization of translation, and indirectly its industry. The West itself is just opening up to the excitement of translation studies, which, announces Mona Baker, is the discipline of the nineties (1998). Through the discussion below, I have attempted to historicize the present moment. What follows is a rapid outline of a few key developments in translation theory in the West.

Translation studies today, are "international" as also "interdisciplinary" (Venuti, 2000). Theories of translation in the West have over the years, but especially since the 70s, undergone a radical change. The peripheral standing of translation theory in the past could not have foreshadowed the vigour and energy that characterizes the discipline today (especially after Translation Studies became an independent discipline in the eighties). Translation theory and practice have become central to literary studies in the West. Translation scholars generally agree upon the breaking away of translation from an exclusively linguistic exercise to its recognition as a complex cultural practice, as the point of departure. The 'polysystem theory' by Evan-Zohar (1998, 2000) and Toury (1998, 2000) exemplifies a decisive advance in translation research. The linguistic slant of the previous decades did generate a certain degree of 'scientisation' and established translation as much more than a dilettante activity. However, the polysystem theory for the first time raised questions regarding location and reception in relation to the wider scheme of literary forms and genres. The expansions in translation research, set off largely in the 60s 70s, began to be defined in disciplinary frameworks after the 1980s. Hence, Bassnett made a "timely intervention" through *Translation Studies* ((1980) 1991). The refusal to see translation as embedded in the political ideology has been stridently critiqued in the writings of Andre Lefevere (in Venuti, 2000) and Theo Hermans (1985) in the eighties. Close on their heels came Lori Chamberlain's perspective on gender (in Venuti, 2000) (which paved the way for scholars such as Barbara Godard (1986) and Sherry Simon (1996)) in 1988, and marked the beginning of translation's alliance with feminism. Similarly Eric Cheyfitz (1991) and Vicente Rafael (1988) injected issues of colonialism in translation theory. In the meanwhile, the poststructuralist effect on translation theory was made visible by commentaries (see Niranjana, 1992; Venuti, 2000) on Walter Benjamin and Paul De Man's essays on translation, recuperated for postcolonial and poststructuralist agenda. Spivak's essay on the "Politics of Translation" (1993) imbued by perspectives of gender, post-structuralism and postcolonialism acts as a pivot and is an illustration of the interdisciplinary movement of translation theory in the West, articulated by an Indian, no less.

The interdependence between theory and practice is always a tricky issue, and by establishing a one-to-one correspondence we run into the danger of over-simplification. At the same time, I wish to see theory and practice represented in an equation of consensus-and-market. The foregrounding of translation as an imperative, complex and by no means inferior activity carried out through theory today, helps evolve a theoretical consensus about translation. By the 'practice' of translation I refer to the activity, rather than the act of translation. A cursory look at catalogues and review journals is sufficient to show the increasing number of translations taking place from Indian languages. This actual rise in production represents a view of the market, an assumption that translation is financially and culturally viable, or hopes to be. Thus revisions in the theoretical stand also coincides with greater production and the two support each other. The phenomenon is fairly complex and, as mentioned earlier, cannot be simplified in terms of a demand and market situation. There are also ideological differences in the way English translation activity is perceived. However, some recent developments in the academia, especially in English studies, listed below, point to why English translation may have acquired firm legitimacy today.

English Studies

Typically, a large number of translations in India today, emerge from departments of English. Bilingual or multilingual teachers of English turn to their native skills, especially now that translations have acquired an academic respectability. A cursory look at India's well-known translators shows that they have been teachers of English. This by itself does not become a significant fact. After all, the teaching and studying of English does give translators inwardness with the target language. However, in recent years, the revised perception of translations in the academia has contributed both to its production and absorption by the academic circles. Curricula in many universities reflect not only the institutionalization of translation; but also ensure its sales. Before we see the curriculum as a market, which it certainly is, it is important to take a quick look at shifts in the discipline of English studies.

English studies have always been a colonial legacy, but this fact began to be expressed (or felt?) much more acutely after the eighties. After the eighties many teachers of English in India began to articulate a sense of alienation and anger at having to teach a language and literature imposed upon them. The divorce between a subject interpellated by English studies and the lived-in realities of India found expression through studies like *Rethinking English* (ed. Swati Joshi, 1991), *Lie of the Land* (ed. Rajeshwari Sundar Rajan, 1992) and *Subject to Change: Teaching in the Nineties* (ed. Susie Tharu, 1998). This phenomenon of interrogating the content and substance of English studies cuts across both Anglophone and non-Anglophone parts of the world, but acquired different emphases at each place. If Gauri Viswanathan traces its origins in the history of imperialism (1989), Spivak suggested ways of "interrupting" its "pure enterprise" (1993). Different alternatives to Anglo-American texts also emerged as a result of this debate and the crumbling of the English canon made room for texts from ex-colonies, black and dalit narratives. New paradigms were sought, dissolved and redefined, facilitating reformulations in literary studies. One of the alternatives, at least in the English studies of India, that seems to satisfy many quarters, is Indian texts in English translation. According to Meenakshi Mukherjee (1992), it is one of the ways of investing the teaching of English with relevance and meaning. For teachers of literature, teaching texts from different regions became a new excitement, for those interested in language-teaching, translation served as a pedagogical tool. The slight shifts in the Anglo-American canon had made room for Commonwealth literature and IWE after the seventies. The decades after the eighties, for the moment at least, belong to ILET. Rukun Advani notes the impact of this academic shift on the publishing industry by stating:

> The future seems reasonably good, especially because there is repositioning and questioning of the canon in the universities. There is a shift central ground of what was earlier on the margins. Once these shifts are accelerated there will be a larger market for translations. (personal interview, see Appendix 2)

Our search for academic contexts behind the proliferation of translation takes us into an allied discipline – comparative literature. Lakshmi Holmstrom, the well-known translator of Tamil texts, draws attention to "the thrust of modern literary studies in India, and the increasing importance given to comparisons and connections across different Indic languages, and the interest in retracing and retrieving literary histories" (1997:4-5). This, according to her, has contributed to the growth of the translation industry. In fact, any project of comparative studies across different languages owes its substantiation and analysis to translation. It needs to be admitted that as a discipline "Comparative Literature" has not taken a very firm root in India. However, in terms of attitudes held by English teaching faculties, it has shown a change. It also forms a part of the reorganization of the existing literature faculties. Sisir Das advocates teaching of any literature in English and undermining both "linguistic chauvinism" as well as "vernacular obscurantism" (1998:13). Concrete instances of research projects making use of translation for establishing comparative perspectives indicate how comparative literature gravitates towards translations for substantiation. For instance, an anthology of poetry translated from four Indian languages, viz. Hindi, Gujarati, Marathi and Malayalam titled *Tree of Tongues* (Ramak-rishnan (ed), 1999) is claimed by its editor as a "companion volume" to a project on modernism in India. Similarly, Mini Krishnan (former editor, Macmillan) says:

> I set about planning our new series of translations in 1984-85. Before the 90s we had some idealistic leaders who signed up books like Comparative Indian Literature. When I had to publish that I thought to myself, here is critical matter on every genre of sixteen languages but where are the primary texts? And will they EVER be studied unless we bring them into translation? (personal interview, see Appendix 2)

Feminism

Another development that has contributed to the understanding of translation as a complex, political exercise, and also helped the production of texts-in-translation by women writers (and women translators), is feminism. Centres of Gender Studies not only engage in feminist perspective of translation, but also invite research on women writers, made available, if possible, through English translation. Sherry Simon asserts that Gender Studies and translation emerge out of similar institutional contexts – 'Woman' and 'Translation' have been relegated to the same position of discursive inferiority (1996:1). The common context of marginality makes women's writing from relatively tradition-bound or less-privileged parts of the world and available in English translation very appropriate for absorption into gender studies departments. Spivak addresses a feminist translator as a clue to the workings of gendered agency. She sounds a note of caution against an all-embracing global feminism. She employs 'defamiliarizing' techniques to mark out the difference between an 'Alice Walker' and a 'Mahasweta Devi' (1993). A more tangible interlocking of gender and translation is visible in 'small' and 'niche' presses focusing upon women's texts. In India, Stree and Kali for Women undertake translation on a wide scale as a means to access women's voices. Ritu Menon (co-founder, Kali for Women) asserts, "It is undeniable that women have been translated far less than men have, even though they have been writing for as long and as powerfully, albeit against formidable odds" (1998:127). The English translation (2000) titled *Mai* from the Hindi original (1997) (by the same name) published by Kali, is an illustration of this ideological linking of feminism, translation and women's fiction. The woman protagonist's attempt at 'recovering' her mother's voice becomes a metaphor for the translator Nita Kumar, an established social anthropologist herself, as her attempt to make a 'regional' silence speak. Her two-part discussion (in addition to an Afterword) situates the translated text as an entry into history and anthropology. At the risk of overgeneralization, it may be pointed out that ideological contexts within the academia affect, to a certain extent, choices of texts. Anthologies of poetry and short stories by women writers circulate (or aim to) globally, mediated through English, and provide non-unitary, multi-vocal perspective on the discourse of gender. Translation may not even be a direct concern in such projects, and yet it has a role to play. The words of the editor of *Who's Who: Contemporary Women Writers* below illustrate the point:

> In all cases, my objective has been to create a balanced and international representation which does not slight important writers who are lesser known because they do not write in English…that writers have at least one book available in English translation was the other key principle of selection. (Miller, 2001:xix)

Postcolonialism

In our search for why the translation industry has become more prolific today, we also need to take account of postcolonial studies as an important determinant. A wide range of social and political practices outside the Anglo-American academy is shaped by what is currently called 'post-colonialism'. The term 'postcolonial' is a matter of ongoing debate, especially because as Ania Loomba (1998) notes, it is a temporal as well as an ideological marker. The prefix 'post' refers to chronology – the end of colonialism. In this sense it pertains to movements for cultural decolonization in colonies that have been officially and politically decolonized. However, oppositional discourses did exist even within the politically colonized state. Making for further confusion is the fact that the term carries the connotation of 'supplanting' as in the replacement of the colonial by a new world order that has established unequal relationships among 'free' countries. This is not the place to tease out the various meanings that attend on the term. Various studies in India and abroad 'cover' the impetus, conditions and effects of postcolonial studies. My concern is not an epistemological one, but with the way postcolonial approaches generate and foreground non-Western texts. Aijaz Ahmad (1994) comments upon problematic processes by which through selection, translation and circulation of certain texts, certain voices in western universities create a putative canon. Mahasweta Devi's stories come to the western audience through the authority of Spivak's name and belie and change the notion of the 'translator's invisibility'(1995). In a partly facetious vein, Sujit Mukherjee refers to Spivak as the *'dwarpalika'* (female doorkeeper) of Mahasweta Devi in America (1991). As far as Indian audiences are concerned, Mahasweta Devi has been for long a recognized social activist and a literary figure. Her discovery through the 'English' language is a recent phenomenon and unique perhaps for the West and India's own English-reading middle class. At this point it must be qualified that the assimilation of Mahasweta Devi in academic matters in the West does not signify the West's openness to 'regional' writing from India. The West serves as a potential, rather than a real market as far as 'regional literature' in English translation is concerned. Save Tagore, Mahasweta Devi and a few Urdu poets, ILET has, so far, made little impression upon Western readership. Peter Ripken draws attention to a similar indifference towards African literature and considers the situation of African literature in the international marketplace a "deplorable situation" (1991:290). On the other hand, Latin American literature was read with considerable excitement after the sixties. It may be worth comparing the reception (or lack of it) of different literatures to explore why the West has been indifferent to Indian texts in English translation. Harish Trivedi concludes with characteristic asperity, "The Empire translates back all right, but the metropolitan response seems to be that the Empire itself may lump these translations" (1996:52). This phenomenon calls for a comparison with the Indian English novel. Are the Indian novels in English translation obdurately 'regional' and therefore not palatable for consumption in the West? Is there a difference in images of India provided by the two genres? The dynamics of the international marketplace are fairly complex and given my focus, it cannot be dealt with over here. That said, it is important to remember that the presence of strong contingents of Indian students and academics in Western universities has huge implications for teaching institutions in the future. Departments of South Asian studies call for a reconstitution in the light of changing national and ethnic compositions of a university class (Rocher, web article, n.d.). The sociological changes are likely, sooner or later, to impinge on the framing of courses and therefore the potentiality of the West as a market cannot be ignored.

To come back to our discussion on postcolononialism, it has affected to a certain extent a "shift in the balance of literary trade between the First World and the second and the third worlds", so that the First world provides the theory, while 'others', the texts (Mitchell, 1995:476). Absorbed sometimes in the name of South Asian studies, sometimes third world literature and sometime postcolonial studies, texts from India are now poised to be exported in different avatars. To what extent are these formulations a continuation of formerly called Indological/Oriental/Area studies, constitutes an interesting question. The point is that English still remains the mainstay for agenda of recuperation and/or assimilation. Loomba sums up aptly: "The meaning of 'discourse' shrinks to 'text', and from there to 'literary text' and from there to texts written in English because that is the corpus most familiar to the critics" (1998:96). The writers of *Empire Writes Back* do not consider 'regional' texts (even if subversive and resistant) fit for postcolonial scrutiny "until more extensive translations into English from these languages have been produced" (Ashcroft, Griffiths, Tiffins, 1989:122). For the moment, translations into English have begun to figure strongly in the domestic marketplace.

As we turn to an examination of factors outside the academia that provide sanction to the English translation activity in the next chapter, it is crucial to take account of literary traditions which elude any analysis. Texts do arrive by many haphazard ways into other languages and do not necessarily depend only on linguistic and/or systematic efforts of translation. For instance, novels of the Bengali writer, Sharad Chandra Chatterjee travelled from one language into another without much ado, entirely through invisible translators and without any institutional support. They formed a staple literary diet for readers from languages such as Gujarati, Hindi, Marathi and many more. On a more regular note, translations of Western bestsellers circulate freely, and almost every railway stall houses them without being aware of them as translations. Newspapers and magazines rely on an ongoing and unacknowledged industry of translation, especially from English into the 'regional' media. All this points to many instances of continuous, unrecognized and unselfconscious translation. The preoccupation with a relatively self-conscious phase of translation must not obfuscate such untheorized traditions of translation. At the same time, *Translating India* puts premium on the specific sustenance of this activity from teaching institutions, state and private publishing houses and as we shall see in the following chapter, society at large.

5.   Outside the Discipline Machine

This chapter attempts to locate the dynamics and prominence of English language productions, especially ILET in the changing political economy of postcolonial India. It takes the discussion of the proliferation of English translations away from the academic arena and concerns itself with the socio-cultural matrix in India today. As mentioned earlier, paraliterary and literary phenomena are treated in separate units for maintaining focus and do not suggest mutual exclusivity.

Readerships

English translation in India is now a very self-conscious and self-reflexive activity in India. The 'outwork' of translated texts – prefaces, introductions, publishers' notes – are directed at specific audiences. The case of Nita Kumar's translation of the Hindi novel *Mai* mentioned earlier or the fresh translation of Rabindranath Tagore's *Gora* (1997) introduces the reader not only to the text, but also the academic discourse surrounding it. Aimed clearly at the academic market, the framing of translation is intertwined with the needs of the audience. If academics and students form a specialized, but not insubstantial, market for translation, general readers form another non-specialized market. The two segments overlap; not unlike the overlapping of the 'domestic' and international readerships. It is possible to offer some firm observations about specialized readers, largely by belonging to this category and observing the 'uses' to which translation is put, and hence the analysis of 'academia' in the previous chapter. However, general readers of English offer little opportunity for observation and there are few mechanisms for determining popular choices. The English-reading public of India, in particular, is scattered all over the cities and belongs to the so-called "great Indian middle class" (Varma: 1998). Unlike some of the 'major' Indian languages, the English reading public is not concentrated in a linguistic state and therefore, in linguistic terms, it is an "undifferentiated" and "indeterminable" mass (Mukherjee, 2000:190). At the same time, it represents one of the biggest markets for English language books, and English-language television programmes in the world. It contributes in decisive ways to the content and expression of media in India as it also goes along forming itself in and through media. It is important to see what kind of cultural forms engage its attention and reflect its identity for it is in these formulations that the English literature produced in India can be situated. Before we arrive at those connections, it is crucial to draw the political and economic developments of the last twenty years in rapid and broad strokes as a backdrop to the English-speaking readers of India. As mentioned earlier, English readers largely come from the urban class of India and that segment forms the fulcrum of the discussion below.

It has been demonstrated earlier that English translation activity began to show a remarkable increase after the eighties. Since the nineties it has been striding along energetically with focused planning and publicity. The Indian English novel has been registering a dramatic rise in significance since the eighties, a trend that continues even today. Interestingly these literary phenomena run parallel with sweeping changes (described only briefly here) in the economic, political and cultural landscape of India. For instance, the Congress Party, the single largest and most successful political party since the early twentieth century came to be seriously challenged after the 1980s. Posing as the bastion of India's nationalist struggle against the British, the Congress provided the defining image to Indians for many decades after independence. Its breakdown, made possible partly by smaller, 'regional' and caste-based parties and partly by the BJP, disrupted one of the sustaining and unitary notions of India. Whether what emerged from this breakdown has been any less undemocratic or is not the area of concern here; what is important is that in political terms, India came to be imagined in different and varied terms. There appear to be fewer reasons now to think of India in centrist terms, especially as diverse 'regional' groups push for representation (more visibly now) at the national front.

At an economic level, the liberalization process set in motion in the late eighties became a full-fledged programme in 1991. The economic reforms of that year have liberalized large sections of the public sector and officially allowed for the first time free economy. Released in many ways from the constraints of the socialist state and 'License Raj', Indian people (of a certain class, caste and gender, of course) became ready to create and become a global market themselves. Critiques of economic liberalization and globalization from a capitalistic as well as Marxist point of view are in plenty. It is not within my scope to discuss them in any further detail, my concern being with the way global processes intersect with indigenous, especially cultural productions. Globalizing processes not only impinge on cultural productions but also modify our modes of producing and perceiving them. For instance, books are now publicized and sold as "desirable objects", notes Urvashi Butalia (personal interview, see Appendix 2). Improved technology has made the appearance of books far more alluring for individual readers than it was before. Desk Top Publishing has also accelerated the actual process of book publishing. Apart from these material changes, the book trade as a whole is emerging as a glamorous and high-profile industry. Wider dissemination through the print and visual media, and high-profile readings organized in bookshops have redefined the literary marketplace. Surrounded by hype and visibility, fiction in English, serves as an apt illustration of how since the last decade economic matters have been inextricably linked with cultural productions.

Most commonly, globalization means the removal of national boundaries as impediments to the free flow of capital, goods, and services. However, there is another kind of globalization, which could be described as free trade in images and data (Hochshild, 1998, 1235-1238). India has taken unprecedented leaps in information and technology, once again a phenomenon of the eighties.

In late 1999, India's estimated one-and-half million Internet users represented about one percent of estimated world users (Ram, 2000: 266). Satellite channels in English as well as a few 'regional' languages have created what N. Ram calls the "media bazaar" of India. The acceleration and sweep of and access to information that we witness today are unprecedented. The urban middle class, especially the younger generation, takes to all this like fish to water. The size of the Indian market has helped the expansion of Indian media corporations. Facilitated by joint ventures with international media conglomerates, Indian print and visual media continue to take huge leaps on the basis of the rising middle class. This does not imply however, that the Indian class that watches television/ reads English books/ uses the Internet, consumes passively the economic and cultural forms of globalization. In a very interesting study on the impact of satellite channels in India, Thussu (2000) relates the complex negotiations between the local and the global as the Indian middle class responds to the global media. The beginnings of 'regional' channels on the television or 'regional' software programmes for computers are signs of an interesting market economics which forces multinationals to rethink their content in local terms. Insistence on the local also undercuts resistance to the Western, notes Thussu. This negotiation cuts across many cultural forms, taking different emphases each time. The interaction between the 'local' and 'global' cannot be simplified only in terms of 'think locally, act globally'. We will contextualise this issue against the middle class' responses to culture. For the moment, even at the risk of stating the obvious it must be said that there are serious disparities in the distribution of global gifts. Fissures run deep through urban and rural India, between men and women and between classes. But in this as in so much else, the numerical strength of the Indian population undercuts the argument about the limitations of reach. Three things are relevant for our purpose here: Firstly, information technology, as mentioned earlier, has made the production of books easier and less time-consuming. It has also provided a freer circulation of book trade through the Internet. Secondly, the role of English, discussed earlier in the Indian context, has further expanded as a global language. Thirdly, India enjoys a particularly huge share in the emerging 'knowledge economy' on the basis of its strength in numbers as well as its contribution to the technical know-how of computers. Both of these also put India in a position to press its indigenous forms and modify the content of what moves globally.

The primary push towards globalization and liberalization comes from the urban middle-class. Admittedly, only urban citizens do not form the middle class. Select sections of rural communities also, through economic reforms for rural India and socio-cultural choices, are part of the middle class. Moreover, the Indian city, as Khilnani notes, is the bloated receptacle of every hope and frustration reared by half a century of free politics and exceedingly constrained and unequal economic progress. What is important to note is that Indian cities pervade and expand with the relentless process of urbanization. More than a quarter of all Indians live in cities, some 250 million people, and it is estimated that by

2010 the figure will exceed 400 million, giving India one of the largest urban populations in the world (ibid:109). The fact remains that pre-modifiers such as 'urban' and 'middle' are teasers as they evoke conflicting definitions. Economists prefer to use the term 'consuming' class, while sociologists perceive them as anything but monolithic. It is important to clarify what is meant by the urban middle class here: we refer to that segment of the population that dwells in cities, feels comfortable speaking (and perhaps reading) English and also has the money and inclination to buy books. Unlike the developments outlined earlier, the existence of this class is not a recent one, although it has expanded further in recent times. The urbanization of India has been a gradual process, rising from roughly 20 to 25 per cent during the last fifty years. Conjectures about the size of this urban population vary from 200 to 300 million. Assuming that only two per cent (once again the range is between 2 and 5 percent) of this population knows English, "two per cent of Indians are a lot of human beings; they constitute a population of larger than Australia's and New Zealand's put together; both of which are entirely English-speaking" (Yagnik *et al.* 1995:77).

The demographic shift discussed above needs to be juxtaposed with the Indian diaspora, another huge segment for books in English. After the immigration laws of 1965 in the United States, India has witnessed a huge outflow of its educated and skilled citizens. In fact, the effect of the 1965 change in immigration policy has been a decisive one on South Asia as a whole. However, the NRI (non-resident Indian) has had far more implications for economic, political and cultural matters in India than non-resident citizens of any other country. The generation that emigrated after the sixties had knowledge of English (unlike the rural labour of the previous decades). Young, ambitious and upwardly mobile, it formed the first layer of the Indian diaspora, huge and influential today. The children of this generation have now reached early adulthood and are joining the college population in increasing numbers (Rocher, web article, n. d.). Their ways of knowing and accessing India govern many cultural productions, an issue we will revert to later. In the meanwhile, the excitement caused by some of these developments is summed up like this by Gurcharan Das:

> The power of democratic India that has unleashed the market is finally rooted in its ability to make more of its human capabilities than ever before possible. Freeing the individual has released vast resources of energy and creativity. This is now channeled into software, entertainment, remote services, Internet start-ups, as well as Indipop, fashion, cricket mania and Indian novels in English. (2000:377)

Culture and Commerce

We have, so far, situated the English-reading segment of urban India within the multiple contexts of the demographic, political and economic changes of the last two decades. The discussion below centers around the middle class once again, but many observations also include the Indian diaspora. Before any further elaboration, it is important to define what is meant by 'culture' over here. The term 'culture' evokes excessive meanings, and this is not the place to define its finer aspects. For a more sustaining insight into culture, I refer to Bhiku Parekh's definition of culture as "a way of understanding, structuring, conducting and talking about human life and encompassing all that is necessary for this purpose" (1997:165). Parekh defines culture in a fundamental sense, whereas late capitalism reduces culture to things – physical and concrete such as books, films, music, food, places. The last two decades have witnessed the foregrounding of culture as an economic commodity that can be bought and sold. The spurt in translation activity has to be contextualised against this connection between culture and commerce. Before we come to translation proper, it is important to observe the cultural predilections of the Indian middle class (and to an extent, the Indian diaspora).

A closer look at the cultural world of the Indian middle class reveals a loss of literacy in the 'mother tongue' and a concurrent rise in English. The processes of urbanization and migration discussed earlier have led to the loss of literacy in the mother tongue, especially in the second generation. In both cases, that is, emigration from villages to cities within the country, or emigration across borders – the pressures of retaining anything other than the mainstream language are tremendous. Children of linguistic communities settled in spots far from what used to be called 'the native place' can usually speak their 'mother tongue' but they seldom learn to read it. They acquire English, the 'regional language', and in most states, Hindi as well; if in addition a Tamil child has to learn Tamil, the parents have to make special arrangements. A corollary to migration within and across borders is also the gradual breaking away of the joint family system which further adds to a linguistic alienation among the younger generation and increases the odds against retention of the 'mother tongue'. In contrast to the 'mother tongues', English continues to flourish – the middle class has been its mainstay in India. The middle class stood to gain from it in the past and continues to do so. This mutually reinforcing relationship between the middle class and the English language is part of a historical continuity (see Varma, 1998; Ahmad, 1994). However, since the last two decades, two aspects of this relationship stand out, namely, the 'Indianization' of the English language and the confidence and abandon with which the middle class uses it. If the colonial generations submitted to the power of English, the postcolonial generations bend it and use it for their own purposes (see Burde and Krishnaswamy, 1998). This is because as the nature of this relationship has changed, so have the terms. English is still required for upward mobility, perhaps much more so, but it comes now to the new generations without any colonial hang-ups. The effects of this change are visible in the unselfconscious ways by which it intersperses with Indian languages and by which Indian languages colour English. The outcome is what we see in advertisement jingles, captions, newspaper headlines and in some cases, entire news reports on channels such as Zee TV – an indigenized, postcolonial avatar of English. These processes have created native and hybrid varieties of English, the phenomenon known as 'liberation linguistics' among linguists. The 'nativization' of English is a postcolonial event and therefore not unique to India alone. However, its recognition in India as a creative advantage, an edge, especially in the last two decades has led to tremendous confidence in English print and visual productions. It is not surprising, then, that although Raja Rao had exploited the possibilities of 'Indian English,' it did not draw the kind of attention Salman Rushdie did through *Midnights' Children* (1983). Rushdie timed his linguistic risks with circumstances conducive to hybrid varieties of language and culture, whereas Rao was too far ahead of his time. The sense of abandonment that Indian writers display today as they handle and 'control' the English language also stems from the fact that English in India is de-territorialized. Its connection with Britain through books, manners, images has become very tenuous and it no more evokes an English world so integral to the English educated elite of the previous century. This has resulted in a simultaneous occurrence of the expansion of English on one hand and its decreasing anglicization – a phenomenon captured well in the excerpt below:

> In the heart of Bombay, near Flora Fountain (now Hutatma Chowk, or Martyrs' Square) is a popular restaurant called Pyrkes which, in the early sixties, served boiled chicken. The restaurant has changed its menu and begun to serve spicy Punjabi and Mughlai food. Not far away, opposite the Regal cinema, another restaurant had boiled potatoes on its menu until as late as the eighties. The item is no longer on its menu. In the sixties, there were a few cinema houses even in the outlying parts of Bombay – Bandra, Mahim, King's Circle – that screened English movies regularly. They no longer do so. The college where I taught in the sixties used to subscribe to The London Magazine; it doesn't any longer: foreign journals have become too expensive, and apparently there are not enough people interested, even in colleges, in magazines like LM. ...All these are signs that, since Independence, the culture associated with the English language has lost its hold even in the most westernized city in India. And yet, strangely, in the last decade or two, Indian English poetry has made remarkable strides, and experience a sudden, vigorous flowering. (Sarang, 1989:1)

Vilas Sarang's observation, quoted above from his introduction to an anthology of Indian English poetry, points to an apparently paradoxical situation. Falling levels of Anglicization have in fact facilitated literary productions in English. To go a step further, the middle class in India now not only finds English suitable for self-expression, but since the eighties, seeks and creates forms that emphasize Indianness through English. Apologetic statements about writing in English (found in seminars until the eighties) have given way to a robust confidence culminating in Rushdie's claim that only English writings from India deserve attention (1997)! Rushdie's claim is undeniably unfounded, but what cannot be ignored is the way English productions in India, unwelcome and ignored for many years, dominate any literary discourse anywhere now. The prominence is largely created through hype, but at the same time, its importance as a medium for self-expression remains undisputed. It is relevant for us to note that many cultural forms (including productions in English) that engage the middle class in India reflect a certain pattern. These forms created by and for the middle class and the diasporic Indians show an amalgamation of 'regional'/homegrown/bhasha experience with English. The amalgamation itself cannot be simplified in terms of a local content and global expression. (These categories slip and slide into each other, therefore terms such as 'regional' and 'pan-Indian' or 'local' and 'global used here for convenience are not meant to imply binary oppositions). The interaction between the twin ethos is not only linguistic in nature, it takes different emphases and forms with each genre. The apparatus required to make cultural objects 'global' and circulate them internationally ranges from English to technology, the crucial point being to maintain the modes of disseminating information that find approval in the Western world. For instance, Hindi cinema (aiming at any resident and non-resident Indian) takes recourse to multinational media corporations for publicizing its 'events'. The series of mythological and folk stories called the *Karadi Tales*, on the other hand, may not make use of large-sized media corporations for its publicity but relies upon the high profile of its narrators who render the stories in flawless English. The music set to the narration retains local rhythms and fuses them with western instruments unobtrusively, creating thereby a combination neither completely traditional nor entirely modern but 'right' enough to suit the taste of its target audience. The 'fusion' music of Daler Mehndi and A.R. Rahman has the Congo drums and pan-flute on one hand, the tabla and synthesizer on the other. What comes over to audiences is that there is something here for all, and the product is neither completely 'local' in a limited sense nor completely 'foreign' in an alienating sense. The hybrid nature of modern man's existence and the fluidity of geographical boundaries blend with the fluidity of genres, registers, content and languages in the cultural forms today. In this free-floating world of identities, what seems to remain fixed and common is the English language, in some form or the other.

The English Eth(n)ic

The unique nature of cultural forms which gratify the middle class's identity and aspirations, needs to be viewed as a worldwide phenomenon. In a world of free-floating identities caused by cross-border migration and the melting of national boundaries, specificities of culture help create/retain identities. As a result, both constituencies, that is the diasporic Indians as well as the middle class are Janus-faced – they look towards '*desi*' on one hand and an international ethos on the other for sustainable identity-formation. The interaction between the two forces characterizes the contemporary response to global hegemony. Pockets of

Indian immigrant populations in the U.K. and United States, for instance, arduously guard literature and music in their mother tongue to recover a lost inheritance for themselves and their children. If the same products are available in English, the process become easier for both generations and the purpose is still served, after a fashion. Children's books translated from Indian mythology into English, or quick-to-learn packages for learning specific Indian languages illustrate an anxiety for rootedness. This anxiety is not unique only to the diasporic communities, it exists, albeit to a lesser extent, even among the very urbanized middle class Indians living in India. The increasing nuclearization of families and English-medium education are perceived to have caused deracination, which parents try to counter with cultural goods. Also, the backdrop of globalization breeds the desire to 'do well' – a brand of success defined in an internationally competitive ethos. The same backdrop also evokes a reaction of 'difference' and 'otherness'. The attempt to modify the global content through local inputs has cultural-political as well economic implications. In terms of an argument for cultural and political logic, the move towards localization while retaining the global is a defence against an overriding power, especially U.S. hegemony (see Ghosh, 1999). Admittedly, the international culture industry is currently one of the largest and certainly the fastest growing in the world and a refusal to participate in it may appear valid ideologically, but not economically. What cannot be circulated in this international space faces the danger, at least in the mind of the middle class, of languishing in small provinces and sinking without a trace. The economics of any trade today, cultural or otherwise, stems from this recognition. The process of 'local' and 'global' is therefore a two-way process and eludes simplified understanding implied in the dictum of local content and global expression.

Underlying the Indian middle class' response to a 'globalizing' culture also lies the idea of India as a multilingual and multi-ethnic society. While it is true that we have always, or at least since Nehru, been aware of the cultural diversity of India, it seems safe to say that the last fifteen years have witnessed a frenetic upsurge of 'regional' images seeking to coalesce into a mosaic, a whole, that is India. The metaphor of a 'mosaic' provides a defining image to the producers and consumers of cultural products. India was always a multicultural country, much before multiculturalism began to appear as a fashionable trend the world over. However, it, in the words of Peter D'Souza, was 'multiculturalism by accident'; a situation that happened to have been made up of diverse elements. It did not reduce linguistic and cultural insularities in the manner of 'multiculturalism by design', which is what Peter D'Souza makes a plea for (quoted in Bharucha, 2000:76). It is difficult to say if the present 'interest' in ethnically diverse elements has this component of human openness, but on the whole it appears that 'multiculturalism', 'authenticity' and 'diversity' are concepts that sell well. The middle class reflects upon its own diversity through cultural forms, and both government-aided institutions as well as media corporations provide it with such images of diversity. A very successful television programme called 'Surabhi' aired regularly in the nineties gave 'interesting' details about India to the Indian middle class. Ethnic (now that 'ethnic' is chic) food festivals organized by posh hotels in the metropolitan cities draw the middle and upper-classes. Such forms create self-reflexive ways of 'thinking about India' among the middle class which if in possession of global apparatus (English, technology, publicity), also attracts the West. A critical comprehension of these images shows the presence of state agenda in some and/or market forces in other agencies. Diversity, which Bharucha (ibid:73) refers to as "the most reassuring of cultural categories", involves several selection processes. As different linguistic and ethnic communities draw attention to their cultural 'uniqueness,' culture itself becomes a scramble for self-representation. The last chapter in this study will demonstrate this in the context of English translation activity.

Unity and Diversity

In the meanwhile, emerging from and substantiating the contexts outlined so far, cross-cultural exchanges in cuisine, music and textiles surround us as signs of a pervasive cultural excitement, within in the ripples of which literature can also be located. We turn once again to the specific case of English translation from Indian languages. To continue with our analysis of the English translation activity that proliferates today, we need to examine modes of 'framing' translations in books and anthologies, as well as those of reviewing and receiving them. This involves studying the imagery of translation in newspapers, publishers' notes, blurbs and review journals aiming at general readers. It is interesting to see how introductions and schema in anthologies of poetry and short stories reflect the twentieth century definition of India as a rich, polylingual and multilingual country. In the meanwhile, emerging from and substantiating the contexts outlined so far, cross-cultural exchanges in cuisine, music and textiles (and now literature in English) surround as signs of a pervasive cultural excitement.

The introduction to a Katha collection of short stories says:

> There is so much diversity in Indian stories and often it is the very diversity that loops them together, sensuously, delicately, almost invisibly into something that looks whole to the outsider who does not see the woof and the warp, the brilliant colours that have been cajoled into each and every fibre by varying hands and minds. (Dharmarajan, 1998)

Although this refers to the stories, each story represents in the scheme of the anthology a community, a group, a language, all of which, when bound together, re-create the metaphor of the 'mosaic', discussed earlier. If that came from an introduction by the publisher herself, the reviewers and contributors also employ a similar rhetoric. For instance, Ashish Sharma (8th Feb., 1998) in his review

of a collection of short stories remarks, "Katha volumes are an accessible celebration of the Indian experience in all its diversity". This imagery of diversity
is not unique to the publications of Katha (an organization devoted to Indian
short fiction in English translation). In an anthology titled *India: A Wealth of
Diversity*, the introduction and visuals focus (like brochures of tourism) on the
fascinating mix of voices that constitute India. The project, according to the
editors, is an attempt to "work it out", and "to discover what is happening in the
literature, on the land and within the people in India who, as always with literature, constitute its subject and its center" (Ringold, Editor's Preface, 1999,
Nimrod).

The synonymy of land and literature strengthens the links between the
publishing and the tourism industries, both of which rely on cross-border movements of people and ideas and have been very active since the mid-eighties.
Anthologies of poetry and especially those of fiction (the most popular genre
even in translation), serve as convenient, compact kits for accessing India – an
anthologized, diversified India. In recent years, movements towards more specific and hitherto marginalized voices of India (gay/lesbian, dalit, women,
partition) have added more layers to the industry of translation anthologies.

To come back to modes of marketing translations, some publishers employ
an imagery of brotherhood, suggestive of a traditional, liberal humanist way of
looking at translation. The Sahitya Akademi and the National Book Trust, communicate through their translation projects, a state ideology for resolving
linguistic and cultural differences. The Macmillan series of Indian Novels in
English Translation, the first systematic approach to fiction translation, states
(through the preface) its aim of creating an ongoing sense of an 'Indian tradition':

> Whatever our quarrels and shifting factions, all Indians know that they
> have a complex, stable system of values, beliefs and practices which forged
> long ago has never really been interrupted. Our programme of translation
> is an exploration of this Indian tradition, which is one of humankind's most
> enduring attempts to create an order of existence that would make life both
> tolerable and meaningful. (Mini Krishnan, Editor's Preface, 1997)

The ethical overtones of the passage above are not infrequent even in discussions and ordinary conversations on translation. Frequent use of 'should' and
'must' for 'reading translation so that we know each other' add a moral colour-
ing to the activity. Since knowledge, at least for the upwardly mobile middle
class, is acquired largely through English, it serves as an aid in the 'moral gesture' of countering linguistic and regional chauvinism. The gesture may be
directed at painting a broad picture of India in translation, or more specific traditions of a region or ideology. For instance, an ambitious set of volumes of
translation from Indian languages is tellingly titled *Knit India through Literature* (2000). If the knitting is, even for the Sahitya Akademi that did not recognize
creative efforts in English till the sixties, done through English, differences are
also emphasized through English. So the editors of Women Writing in India

claim that they have:

> tried, therefore, in the translations, not always successfully, to strain against the reductive and often stereotypical homogenization involved in the process. We preferred translations that did not domesticate the work either into a pan-Indian or into a universalist mode, but demanded of the reader a translation of herself. (Tharu and Lalitha, 1993, I:xxii)

The observations made so far draw excessively from publishers' and editors' notes and may be considered as a partial (and vested) point of view. It is important to critically comprehend marketing frameworks for they mirror the dynamics of a literary marketplace. At the same time, it is equally important not to over-emphasize any one segment for arriving at a comprehensive understanding of how cultural products work. Therefore, we now turn briefly to reviews of texts in translation that also employ, very often, thickly textured words for description. A smattering of terms such as 'authentic', 'genuine', and 'real' evoking moral judgment are commonly found in reviews in newspapers and review journals. Another set of metaphors employed in the service of ILET suggest a rich discovery by expressions such as 'treasure-trove', 'wealth', 'gems', and 'pearls'. In his review of the Macmillan series of novels, V. Abdulla refers to the "gems of creative writing nestling in the dark unfathomed oceans of Indian literature" brought to light through translation (1995:59-60). Translation theorists have begun to question the fluffy romanticism as well as indifference to the act of translation evident in reviews of translation and stress the need for revising reviewing systems (see Simon and Viswanatha, 1999).

English translations from Indian languages have begun to figure in critical debates focused on IWE. The spectacular success and prominence of the Indian English novel in the West has invited strong reactions among some writers and critics in India, (see Deshpande, 2000; Sunder Rajan, 2001; Satchidandan, web article, n.d.), who question the politics of representation. Satchidanandan notes that the publicity and visibility of IWE is incongruent with its ability to "portray our social and spiritual lives", and only by making Indian literature available in English can the "hegemonic" role of IWE be countered. Sunder Rajan (2001) points to a feeling common among Indian writers that they have not received their "just desserts" and therefore an active translation industry may work towards restoring that balance.

Reviews, articles, introductions, shape as well as reflect readership patterns. The gamut of opinions presented so far indicates an overall readiness and positive approach towards English translation. It is interesting to note that the age-old objection about the inadequacy of the English language to convey the Indian ethos is hardly ever an issue now. Resulting partly from the nativization of English and partly from the availability of competent translations, English translation activity encounters very few objections. Nirmal Verma, (in Mukerjee and Abhilash, 1999:16) the well-known Hindi writer, attributes some of this to

IWE which has created modes and conventions for a liberating idiom and shaped reading habits. Translators and editors retain cultural-bound terms and sometimes flaunt them without making concessions. Publishers, editors, translators and to an extent, readers, are opening themselves up to new ways of writing and translating into English and thereby interrogating the colonial assumptions of the English language. The standard of "a creative translation" with "a balance of English with good wholesome vernacular cargo" (Rao, 1997:18) fits into the range of cultural products that have both a local as well as global orientation.

The near-total acceptance of an English literary product like translation is a striking contrast to the heydays of anti-English bellicosity when nationalists considered writing in English a suspicious act. English translation was too insignificant to figure directly in the raging battles between those who wrote in English and those who wrote in the Indian languages. Aparna and Vinay Dharwadker (1997, 247-262) note how Indian English writers and their counterparts in the Indian languages fought out a nationalistic battle in the post-colonial sphere over the place of English in literary and cultural systems, till almost the mid-seventies. A residue of that debate continues to exist in reservations about the Indian English novel being too urban and elitist. In fact, translation is spared from such charges by being rooted in original texts that may hail from any section of society. It is a 'golden mean' – it is real and authentic because written in the languages of the masses and expressive of the non-metropolitan experience. The tinge of guilt associated with English is contained within the framework of 'authenticity'. Therefore even those keen to emphasize the elitism and dominance of the English language, do not find literary productions in English translation elitist. The nationalists' charge that English drives a wedge between Indian languages is well and truly countered by its role as a link between Indian languages. In such a scenario, English performs the nationalist role of bringing languages and literatures closer! Rivals have become allies – the opposing camps of the 'English elite' and the so-called 'vernacular nationalists' enter into the mutually convenient pact of translation because translation benefits both groups. The colonizer's language, in this case, can be used to serve the colonized culture (Satchidandan: web article, n.d.).

6.   Publishers' Perspective

See patient Wilkins to the World unfold
What'ver discovered Sanskrit relics hold
But he performed a yet more noble part
He gave to Asia typographic art
(in Kesavan, 1985:264)

Various segments, from many social levels, justify through their reception, the intellectual and cultural cost of a literary product and 'explain' its proliferation. The preceding chapters have shown how a 'literary' product, in this case an Indian text in English translation, is neither confined to, nor exclusively dependent on literary factors alone. Among institutions that canonize works of art, the publishing industry plays a very crucial role. Situated at a point of intersection between culture and commerce, print capitalism 'determines', to an extent, the production and consumption of literature. Publishing choices stem from both cultural and market-driven forces. When it comes to literature, we do not, on the whole, think of market forces as decisive in the generation, availability and reading of books. Of course, books are products of negotiations between publishing agencies and socio-cultural trends. In the complex interplay of demand and supply, readers' desires are both created and addressed, making the role of publishing and disseminating too important to ignore. This part of the study is based on the premise that the proliferation of books in English translation in the recent decades and the dynamism of English-language publishing in India are interconnected. As in the earlier chapters, the main focus of this chapter is the period of the mid-eighties. What follows here, therefore, is a discussion of the preceding period.

An Historical Introduction

Printing and publishing began systematically with the British presence in India, although the Jesuit missionaries had made sporadic efforts at printing, or more precisely, at spreading the Gospel through print, in the 1550s. Printing, as we know it today, began when in 1706 Bartholomew Ziegenbalg, the well-known Protestant missionary, started working with a printing press in Tranquebar. A little later the East India Company installed a press at Vepory, a suburb of Madras. Sir Eyre Cooke printed his own work, a Malabar and English Dictionary in 1779. These early attempts at printing were occasional and without the typography unique to each language. However, they still laid an important foundation for the all-pervasive development of printing that took place by the middle of the nineteenth century.

Sisir Kumar Das notes that the establishment of the Serampore Mission Press stabilized scattered exercises in printing and publishing (1991:32). Started by Joshua Marshman, William Ward and William Carey in 1800, the Serampore Mission Press may be considered a watershed in the movement from the scribal to the printed word. The Serampore Mission Press initially published translations of the *Bible* into different Indian languages. Gradually the press began regular production of dictionaries and English translations of religious and literary masterpieces in Sanskrit and Persian. It also began publishing the works of English officials who had come to Serampore College and Fort William College for training. In the meanwhile, the British with the help of local experts had begun to invent language types for many eastern languages. These types first appear in Halhed's *A Grammar of the Bengal Language* in 1778. Charles Wilkins' contribution in this regard has been very remarkable. Wilkins was mentioned as a translator in the first chapter, but it is his contribution to typography that earned him his place in the annals of history. Thus, on the whole, printing had made inroads into most Indian languages by the end of the nineteenth century. The course was slow, steady and far from uniform in all languages.

From printing in the Indian languages let us turn our attention to printing specifically in English. While regional presses owned and run by Indians flourished in British India, publication activity in English during the nineteenth century and the first few decades of the twentieth century was, by and large, in the hands of the British. Exceptional cases like Rajpal and Sons, or M.N. Roy's Renaissance Publications or Gandhi's Navjivan Press (one of the first bilingual presses in the country), did not alter the scene which continued to be dominated by the British. Fringe efforts like that of the indigenous firm Popular Prakashan (1928), which also published English books were overshadowed by the large-scale operations of the British firms. Macmillan, Longman and the Oxford University Press (established in 1903, 1906 and 1912 respectively) were the only ones to meet the demand for English textbooks in India. Until 1947, India's entire English language book trade and most of its publishing industry comprised titles imported from the U.K. Indians confined themselves to subsidiary activities like distributing, importing and reprinting books (Altbach, 1975; Kumar, 1998; Menon, 1998). At this point we need to take account of two landmark developments in the fifties – the establishment of the Sahitya Akademi (1954) and the National Book Trust (1957). These public sector undertakings have had the responsibility of 'nation-building' by making knowledge available to all sections of the society. In the fifties, full-fledged and commercial publishing activity by private firms was a tall order, given the absence of a market and the socialist leanings of the nation-state. However, we see some glimmerings of this kind of activity in the Asia Publishing House in the sixties and in P. Lal's Writer's Workshop. The government's decision to nationalize school textbooks in the sixties was a serious blow to the very few English-language publishers operating in India. Textbooks, 'guides', and ancillary materials constitute what is called 'educational' publishing which form the backbone of English-language publishing in India. Textbooks in particular provide stable and mass sales to institutions and libraries. The nationalization of textbooks, implemented with a view to subsiding textbooks and reducing the gaps between the elite and the masses, altered the structure of the publishing industry irrevocably. Some publishers veered towards areas of general interest (fiction, poetry, travel and autobiographies) and tried addressing the individual buyer. This phenomenon, called 'trade' publishing, is germane to the issue at hand in that it provides the context of literature publication. The attempts made by Jaico and Vikas in the sixties to publish titles in fiction and poetry by Indian authors need to be contextualized against this move towards trade books. Such sporadic and scattered efforts at publishing English-language books characterize the sixties, seventies and some part of the eighties also. Indiscriminate import of foreign books, remaindered titles and rigid government policies assailed the book business in India. Along with all this, the size of the English-reading public never made English-language publications commercially viable. The small section that did read in English mostly read English authors or European authors in English translation.

Post-eighties Scenario

The last ten to fifteen years have seen a number of changes in the publishing scenario, some dramatic while some not so dramatic. A broad overview of the situation will bring these to light. While the industry may still be viewed in terms of the private and public sectors there have been changes in the structuring of English-language publishing on the whole. On the one hand public–sector publishing agencies have upgraded their English language publications, and on the other private publishers have extend their interest to areas traditionally considered the domain of the public sector. While this overlapping of roles has created competition at one level, it has also strengthened the industry by tie-ups and collaborations at another. The opening-up of India's economy after the eighties has caught the attention of multinational publishers. "A lot of foreign publishers have come seeking the world's largest English-knowing and reading (if not actually buying) audience. They have found it a very price sensitive market and they can only hope to make up in volume what they cannot achieve through high prices" (Krishnan, personal interview 1998). The growth of the English-reading market is visible today, not only in terms of the number of books but also in terms of an expansion of segmented and niche markets. Given the size and cultural preoccupations of the middle class (discussed earlier), English books by Indians make cultural as well as economic sense today. Foreign books not only fail to answer the specific postcolonial needs of an Indian reader, but are also prohibitively expensive since the devaluation of the Indian rupee. The broad context of English-language publishing in India as well as the post-eighties' shifts helps us understand the 'boom' of the Indian English novel and the rise of ILET today. As things stand now, educational publishing still constitutes about 80 per cent of English language publishing in India. The space created for trade books though, however small, is far from insignificant. Indian publishers tap the indigenous market for literary, academic and specialized books. Consequently, publishing firms such as Oxford University Press, Permanent Black, Sterling, Papyrus, Prestige, Pencraft and Sage for academic books; Kali for Women and Stree for gender studies; Rupa-HarperCollins, Ravi Dayal, Indiaink for books of literary and general interest and many more, define the publishing scene. The last twenty years have witnessed the emergence of more players than ever before. Run by professional and enterprising editors, both old and new Indian publishing firms confidently face the English-language market and target its various segments.

It can be concluded from the above that many factors have contributed to the optimistic mood in the Indian publishing industry today. To begin with, a consistent devaluation of the rupee against the dollar has made imported books prohibitively expensive. The cheapest imported books are virtually unaffordable for the average Indian buyer. After the eighties, this created a small vacuum which Indian publishers have been trying to fill with books produced in India. This economic development has coincided with the increase in trade publishing – which means publishing geared towards an individual reader and focusing upon popular fiction, literature in translation and books of general interest. Traditionally, 90 per cent of Indian publishing has been educational; it has always addressed institutional buyers – all sales have been library sales. There is now a significant shift from institutional to individual buyers, which in turn means that the individual reader needs to be continuously informed about books available in the market. Almost all the leading newspapers in the country carry a page on new 'literary titles'. Reviewing books has become a regular, on-going activity with the appearance of journals such as *The Book Review, The Indian Review of Books* and *Biblio* devoted almost exclusively to reviews. Television plays its part by telecasting interviews with new authors. Promotion and publicity, integral features of trade books, have made books very visible today. Narendra Kumar concludes his evaluation of the current publishing scene by commenting that for the first time, "the industry is being professionalized to an extent that the nineties opened new vistas which could lead to the full flowering of Indian scholarship in the best sense of the term" (1998:1). The professionalization of the industry has resulted in better editorial standards and focused marketing, which has to a certain extent led to an 'image make-over' of books, turning them into consumer products. The visibility may not always translate into sales, it may not, in fact, even increase economic investment in books, an issue we shall revert to. For the moment, the discussion moves from a broad overview of developments in English-language publishing to the specific trajectory of English translation.

The Cultural Economics of English Translation

Though government-funded bodies like the Sahitya Akademi and the National Book Trust may appear less relevant in these times of late capitalism, they are still useful in many ways. They reach out to languages and genres that do not attract private publishers. Also, since their stakes are low they can afford to venture into fresh pastures. When we turn to the case of English translation proper, the subsidized activity of the Akademi, which included translation for the first time, has a very significant contribution. It marked, according to Menon (1998), the first phase of translation and made it possible to create an initial corpus of literary works. Though the usefulness of the Sahitya Akademi and the NBT cannot be gainsaid, their commitment to quality and their modes of distribution have been far from satisfactory. Private publishing houses, on the other hand, could have afforded editorially sound translations along with efficient systems of distribution. However, the small size of the English reading public acted as a deterrent to private publishers, and hence for a very long time, publishing translation came to be seen as an uneconomical activity that is primarily 'good for the nation'. Outside the framework of the institutions just mentioned, first Jaico and Hind Pocket Books and later Sangam Books (Orient Longman), Vikas, Arnold Heinemann, Oxford University Press and Bell Books brought out Indian authors writing in English and translated into English. According to Menon, this marked the second phase of translation and was characterized by "an improvement in distribution and marketing and much greater attention to the quality of translation" compared with the earlier state-subsidized activity (2002:124). Some of the best known works were translated in this period, although translation did not have a huge readership. Jaico brought out the translation of Premchand's *Godan*. Vikas alone published over thirty titles which include Bhisham Sahni's *Tamas* (as *Kites will Fly*) and Kiran Nagarkar's *Seven Sixes are FortyThree*. Bell Books published Krishna Sobti's *Blossoms in the Darkness*, Indira Parthasarthy's *River of Blood* and some others. Oxford University Press, in addition to some titles in Indian English literature, also brought out influential works in translation. The series of Indian Drama in English introduced Girish Karnad, Vijay Tendulkar, Mohan Rakesh and Badal Sircar and paved the way for a 'National Theatre'. A fairly substantial body of translations from Tamil, Kannada, Marathi, Bengali and Hindi was created, but on the whole, translation was not commercially viable. Menon maps the third and current phase of translation announcing that "quantitatively as well qualitatively there is a sea-change"(1995:16). Since 1986 the Akademi has been organizing workshops on literary translations at the national and regional levels. The Akademi is now concerned with all the aspects – theoretical, cultural and practical – of translation activity. It has created a pool of translators whose names appear in the *Translator's Directory*. In 1996, the Akademi also set up a centre for translation that functions as a resource centre for all kinds of translation across the country. It also plans to bring out the first-ever and the most comprehensive history of translation in India. Katha, a non-government organization set up in 1988, is equally, if not more, committed to translation. Its programme Kathavilasam is geared towards the institutionalization of translation theory and practice. Like the Akademi, Katha also conducts workshops, seminars, institutes awards and forms advocacy groups to improve the lot of translation activity in India. The high-profile nature of Katha's activities have gone a long way in making the general public aware of the importance of translation. As part of the Katha Translation Contests, it invites literary experts to nominate a 'good' but untranslated story which is sent out to contestants all over the country. A panel of distinguished writers and critics judge the quality of translation and in a well-publicized event, prizes are awarded for the best translation. The anthologies of stories emerging out of these events have done extremely well in the domestic market – they run into frequent reprints. Unlike the Sahitya Akademi and Katha, niche publishers like Kali for Women and Stree (established in 1984 and 1990 respectively) are indirectly involved in the activity of translation. Committed to the ideology of gender, both Stree and Kali publish women's texts (fiction, autobiographies, non-fiction), and in the process, resort to English translation. Although translation figures only as a means to a different ideological end, these publishers publish at least ten works in translation each. Stree also has an imprint called Samya, devoted to issues of caste and untouchability and this also takes recourse to English translation. The three prominent educational publishers of India – Macmillan India, Orient Longman and the Oxford University Press have increased space for English translation over the years by either reviving their old series or introducing new ones. Apart from publishing well-known dramatists like Vijay Tendulkar and Girish Karnad, the OUP has also published novels like U.R. Ananthamurthy's *Samskara* and Gopinath Mohanty's *Paraja*. Presently, OUP plans to introduce a fresh series of Modern fiction in translation. Macmillan published its first translation in 1978 and till about the mid-nineties, the list of its works in translation never went beyond five to six translated works. However in 1996, Macmillan introduced the very ambitious programme of Modern Novels in English Translation (MINT) and under this programme, it has brought out about eighty works in fiction. Translation had become a part of Orient Longman's publishing programme in the 70s with a series titled Sangam. Despite the Herculean efforts of the editors, the series was discontinued for lack of a market. In these changing times, Sangam is reborn in the avatar of Disha, an imprint of Orient Longman that includes Indian English writing as well as translation. Large-sized commercial publishers like Penguin India (set up in 1985) and Rupa-Harper Collins (tie-up in 1991) tap the Indian market for IWE and topics of general interest. Even so, their interest extends to English translation – Penguin India publishes at least fifteen titles in translation annually, while Rupa-HarperCollins publishes five. The increasing interest in translations evident in new titles makes today's juncture an important one. Meenakshi Mukherjee sums up the publishers' involvement very aptly:

> What we now witness is the emergence of a systematic and promotional production by institutions and established publishing houses who carefully select the text to be translated; control the quality and texture of the translation; provide a suitable context for each book, introductions, translator's prefaces and notes. (1998:34)

It should be evident from the above that the English language industry is abuzz with activity and the excitement of exploring native talent through English is spilling into the area of regional languages also. Undoubtedly the purpose of outlining this trajectory was to communicate the 'contribution' of the publishing industry and identify it as one of the key institutions that provides concrete and external attention to English translations. At the same time, the word 'contribution' suggests an unproblematic and benign relationship, and not the complex process of negotiating between culture and commerce that the publishing industry is actually engaged in. In an age of print capitalism, institutions of print and visual media wield enormous power and influence as far as cultural perceptions are concerned. They may focus only hegemonic forms of culture and reinforce hierarchies, or alternatively they may walk the tight rope between politically correct choices and economic considerations. Some of these tensions and resolutions are visible even in the case of English translations. For instance, Oxford University Press's recent publication of the first novel from Konkani into English (*Upheaval* by Pundalik Naik, trans. Vidya Pai) is indicative of its decision to support and foreground a historically marginalized language. Similarly, Katha's encouragement to all languages, written as well oral, for its anthologies of short stories is also borne out of a publisher's choice to include an ethical component in an economic proposition. *An Anthology of Tribal literature* (ed. G.N. Devy, 2002) by Penguin India also marks a departure in publishing concerns. However these are exceptions, or rather the glimmerings of a new beginning by way of which the print media is making India's (ironically newly-discovered) linguistic diversity a truly marketable object. Be that as it may, publishers of translations are governed by affiliations, for personal or popular reasons, with certain languages and we shall examine this issue now. To start with, the Sahitya Akademi has always perceived translation as a 'unifying' tool between linguistic communities. Its express aim of providing 'uniform representation' to each language may be seen in its preference for 'representative' and canonized texts for translation. The Akademi's list of 'recognised' languages is more inclusive than that of the Eighth Schedule, and it publishes from dialects and 'minor' languages also. It forms Advisory Boards from each language, which recommend texts in order to ensure equal representation. The Akademi is not always able to fulfill this task (an issue examined later), but the fact remains that it is bound by considerations of uniformity, a limitation not known to private publishers. Private publishers prefer source texts only from 'prestigious' and therefore marketable languages like Bengali and Hindi. It was mentioned earlier that Katha, has been able to include a couple of stories from dialects and marginalized languages and does claim to be free of the "politics of languages and representation" (Dharmarajan, personal interview, 1998). Admittedly Katha engages in the publication of short stories, and so can afford to add variety to its anthologies without risking the commercial viability of an entire book. Penguin India, Rupa-HarperCollins and Ravi-Dayal restrict themselves to only well-known authors from widely accepted languages. Traditionally, Oxford University

Press has also refrained from venturing into less known texts and languages. Thus languages like Bengali, Malayalam, Tamil, Telugu and Kannada figure in commercial efforts but 'minor' languages such as Manipuri and Kashmiri hardly ever do. The preference for certain source languages also rests upon the availability of in-house editors in each publishing house. Editors in publishing houses select or commission a work of translation. In a cost-effective scenario, reviews of translations by outside reviewers increase cost and, therefore, editors are obliged to select from among languages that they know. Representatives from Penguin India and Rupa-Harper Collins state that their publishing house also publishes texts recommended by in-house editors. Stree admits of having a very high quality Marathi literature list because Stree's business partner is Popular Prakashan from Mumbai. Thus private publishers choose works in translation depending upon the popularity and acceptance of a SL, its marketability, and the availability of editorial skills. If the Akademi is hamstrung by the burden of non-literary considerations such as uniformity, the private publishers are bound by the "logic of the market" (Satchidanandan, personal interview, 1997). In either case, the para-literary contexts underscore the politics of translation. We notice that publishing philosophies have an impact not only on the languages and texts, but also on the genres of translation. Since fiction is the most popular genre of the present century, we find its preponderance in almost all publishing programmes. Fiction's claim to 'realistically depict various aspects of modern India' (Satchidanandan, web article n.d) makes it more amenable for publication. Trivedi considers this as a trend that "conforms broadly to Frederic Jameson's obviously inadequate and slanted description of Third World literary works as national allegories" (see Trivedi 1996:51-52). Macmillan India entered the arena of translation with its series of Modern Novels in Translation, its aim being to "show as authentic a picture as possible of the different strata of Indian society" (Krishnan, personal interview, 1998). Katha has focused almost entirely on short stories, a commitment born out of the founder's belief that "at the beginning of everything is the story" (Dharmarajan, personal interview, 1998). For those at Katha, the 'story' represents the most organic and primal relationship between human beings and literature. The Akademi, on the other hand, ventures into genres such as poetry, autobiography, travelogue, and literary treatise, which, by and large, seem risky to private publishers. At the same time, Stree and Kali for Women's efforts to examine how knowledge of and by women is created, have taken them to translations of biographies, monographs as well as academic studies. Drama in English translation has remained a much neglected area, a lacuna that Seagull books from Calcutta has attempted to fill. Seagull's manifesto of its series titled New Playwrights of India mentions:

> In a country divided by language, regional traditions and cultural variations, promoting cultural interaction across differences becomes all the more important. In the field of theatre, there was a major gap of knowledge of one another's theatre tradition between the different states. In order to

bridge this gap, translation was perceived as important, translation into a link language common to most states, i.e. English accepted by the south and the north as a practical compromise to enable communication. (www.seagullindia.com).

In its rhetoric of diversity and "cultural interaction", Seagull does not frame its statement of purpose any differently from other publishers. However, its decision to handle a relatively less popular genre makes Seagull's contribution unique.

Do Translations Sell?

In broad terms, all private publishers share a common concern for commercial benefit. At the end of the day, regardless of the nature of the text, every publisher has to decide whether it is economically viable or not. Publishers may differ in their strategies to meet this goal, but in purely business terms, any given book has to at least pay for itself. Generally speaking, the path of English-language publishing is far from smooth. "The English-knowing reader, the backbone of the market, is still scattered over a very wide area and difficult to reach, in the absence of good bookshops in all but the larger cities", notes Ravi Dayal (1998:30-35). In addition to this, competition from other kinds of media such as television, computers, CD- ROMs is disturbingly real, as is the competition from foreign investors. Raising the visibility of books does help but it also creates a 'catch-22' situation, so that books don't sell without publicity (Renuka Chatterjee, personal interview, 1997). The process of exploring these issues brings to light the undeniable fact that publishing translation is far from lucrative. Compared to other kinds of texts that can be priced high or sold in large volumes, translations have small print-runs and are relatively low priced. Mandira Sen (Stree) rightly notes, "Translations, despite the Crossword award, still do not have the 'glamour' of writing in English by Indian" (personal interview, 2001). At the same time, the decision to add new titles and commission works indicates that even as a business proposition, it cannot be written off completely. In order to have translations survive, publishers either have a very selective list or invent strategies and address specific target groups. By focusing upon a specialized market for women's texts, Kali for Women has done well in the overseas market. Stree targets a similar market but prefers to tie up with a foreign agent or sell distribution rights to an overseas publisher. Oxford University Press and Macmillan India continue despite unsatisfactory sales, because texts in translation have potential as textbooks. The Macmillan project, a unique combination of what Sujit Mukherjee calls "private vision and commercial effort" (1997:166), succeeded in countering the lack of viability. In the words of its chief editor:

> The most important item of survival is money. I don't believe that translations are lucrative unless you get one or two titles into university board

> prescriptions every year. Translations rarely pay for themselves. Hence
> our translations are targeted towards home audience, students and foreign
> readers. My concern was how best to make it possible for these transla-
> tions to be both enjoyable reading material and textbook design. (Krishnan,
> personal interview, 1998)

The nexus between academic institutions that help by absorbing texts for students and publishing houses that publish texts is a very crucial one. At this
point, even at the cost of focus, a digression into the relations between translators, academics and publishers needs to be made. Very often, continuities run
from literary practitioners, academics/translators and publishers in the English
language book industry in India. For instance, Rukun Advani (ex-editor, Oxford University Press and currently the founder, Permanent Black) is also the
author of a novel *Beethoven among the Cows*. Pankaj Mishra (founder, IndiaInk)
is the author of the novel *The Romantics*, while David Davidar (CEO, Penguin
India) is the author of a recent novel *The House of Blue Mangoes*. Urvashi
Butalia and Ritu Menon (co-founders, Kali for Women) have also contributed
to literature and personal histories on Partition. In the earlier decades, the well-
known writer Girish Karnad was also the editor of the Oxford University Press,
just as a pioneering translation theorist, Sujit Mukherjee was an editor with
Orient Longman, as was Priya Adarkar, an established translator from Marathi
into English. Such examples are legion, but the tenor of the argument is that
there are continuities and inseparable connections between literary activities
(such as writing and translating) and teaching and research on one hand, and
publishing and editing on the other.

To come back to the subject of selling translations, we must remind ourselves that not all publishers rely upon educational institutions for their clientele.
If Macmillan targets the market for educational books, Katha aims at the common reader and the neo-literate; Kali concerns itself with the market for feminist
texts. Penguin and HarperCollins, on the other hand, aim at a general Indian
readership and confine themselves to titles of general interest. Within India,
Katha volumes have gone into reprints and created ripples in the domestic market. Its focus on stories alone makes a Katha volume easy reading; a feast of
stories for the price of a single book makes it 'good value for money'. Thus,
niche markets, new disciplinary formations, syllabi in schools and colleges – all
these form different mechanisms of countering the cost of publishing a translation. It can be concluded from the foregoing that the body of ILET, however
small, acquires its specific slants from publishing concerns, among other things.
The philosophy of translation differs from one publishing house to another, differences reflected in decisions regarding selections of Source texts, SLs, genres,
and finally the targeting of the market. These decisions usually stem from the
set of explicit or implicit aims and priorities of each publishing house. The implementation of the translation programme of each publishing house is in keeping
with the way it perceives translation vis-à-vis other publishing activities. This is

not to say that goals do not get modified or that publishing programmes are always congruent with the stated goals. In the chapter on Gujarati, we shall see this issue from the point of view of a constituent part of ILET, in itself a pie with unequal pieces from different languages. In the meanwhile looking at the publishing scenario today, this seems to be a good time to be publishing translations. The field is likely to grow more exciting and competitive – a recent strong indication being Picador India's arrival here to tap the Indian market potential not just in terms of writing in English, but translations as well. From the publisher's point of view, it now means "recognizing the importance of quality translations and paying for them; and, simultaneously, developing the market for writing in translation, and translation itself as a desirable skill" (Menon, 1995:16). Copyright policies and revised payments for translators today bear out the recognition extended to translators by the publishing world. With the exception of the Sahitya Akademi which holds the copyrights of all its publications, translators and authors now equally share the copyright. Most publishers provide ten percent royalty to be divided between the author and the translator. Even in cases of a lump sum payment, the amount distributed between the two is equal. The generous space given to translator's introductions and prefaces further testifies to the fact that a translator is now considered important in the scheme of publishing. The difference between a 1954 edition of Rabindranath Tagore's *Gora* in an English translation (which contains a single- line humble acknowledgement by an unnamed "The Translator") and the re-translation of the same book in 2000 with an impressive translator's name and a superb introduction by an established critic, shows that English translation activity in India has come a long way. The very physical appearance and format of a text in translation today indicates the presence of a translator, an entity missing altogether from the pages of many publications earlier.

7.   The Case of Gujarati

> It would be good economy to set apart a class of students whose business
> would be to learn the best of what is to be learnt in the different languages
> of the world and give the translations in the vernaculars. (M.K. Gandhi,
> 1938:9)

> Translation, especially in a multi-lingual country like India, has deep cul-
> tural implications. It is even a measure of the growth achieved by a language
> and also of the dominance of certain languages over others. Even the use
> of certain languages as filter languages for translation into other languages
> involves the question of power. When a work in an Indian language is
> translated into a more powerful national/Indian culture; when made avail-
> able outside India, it involves representing a national culture, which today
> unfortunately means Western culture. (Satchidanandan, 1997:7)

The Jnanpeeth award, (the most prestigious award for literature instituted by
the Government of India and not extended to any Indian English writer to date)
for the year 2001 was conferred upon Indira Goswami from Assam. Undoubtedly all awards and prizes are controversial, especially literary ones since literary
merit is a fuzzy concept. What interests us here are the terms of objections and
explanations voiced by the Gujarati literati on the occasion of this year's award.
In articles included in the Gujarat Sahitya Parishad's journal *Parab* (August
2001), and local newspapers, leading writers such as Bholabhai Patel and Chinu
Modi referred to the role played by English translation in the jury's decision.
According to them, Gujarat's well-known writer Rajendra Shah was also short-
listed for the award but the dearth of his work in English translation made him
lose out to Indira Goswami whose writings are accessible in English. The in-
separability of national recognition and English translation has never been this
unequivocally felt and articulated in Gujarat before. To my mind, the reaction of
the Gujarati literati signifies an important moment in the state's literary history.
It is clear that the frenetic activity of the kind described so far, the claims and
prestige attached to the English language and its potential for (inter) national
dissemination have finally dawned upon the Gujaratis, who have, by and large
remained indifferent to this activity. Another clear signal indicating this is the
fact that Gujarati has more translations to show in the last five years than in the
entire twentieth century. Both the absence of translations earlier and the zestful
efforts to produce translation today, beg scrutiny. The event described above
also throws light on how languages have begun to jostle and rub shoulders with
each other to occupy the space of English translation drawing attention to the
'politics' and internal dynamics of translation.

It must be stated, at the outset, that translation into English necessarily
presumes a set of resources such as a large number of persons, who are bilingual
and who see the need for such translation, the availability of agencies that can

commission or publish translations, and a market for literary works. Bilingualism, in this case of Gujarati and English, relies heavily on levels of competence in English which, in turn, is linked with the educational and cultural legacies of the British. The 'system' as such was not a homogenous one; its implementation and reception differed from state to state and language to language. Devy notes that "the divide in the impact can be seen not only in the obvious terms of 'main centres' and 'hinterlands', but also in terms of individual bhasha cultures" (1992:35). For instance, in Bengal there was considerable Indian support for the new educational system, whereas in Maharashtra the most favoured tendency was to imbibe a Western education through the 'mother tongue'. The emotional, economic and intellectual stakes that each linguistic community had in their relationship with English education also varied from place to place. These regional variations have determined literary production in English in the years that followed, and in some ways they continue to do so today. For instance, by the time Gujaratis started writing in or translating into English, Bengali had already seen two generations use English for creative and polemic purposes. Thus, local configurations play a very important role in determining the activity of translation. In addition to the inequality among languages resulting from historical circumstances such as English education, there are also non-quantifiable, but pervasive perceptions about the 'richness' of some languages (as opposed to other 'not-so-rich' languages), (see K. Satchidanandan, personal interview, Appendix 2), that make translators as well as publishers unwilling to undertake translations from some languages. The case of Gujarati registers a long-standing apathy towards the English language up to the mid-seventies and fervent efforts to compensate for this 'loss' since the eighties. Before we inquire into this shift, it must be borne in mind that linguistic communities in India do not merely emulate or resonate all that happens nationwide, but also respond to their own internal histories and traditions. Equally ungainsayable is the fact that literary traditions operate in a socio-economic context and bear signs of relationships between culture and commerce, between art and everyday life. Hence it is useful to first take a look at native histories of translation in Gujarat and Gujarat's relationship with the English language (a pre-requisite for English translations) shaped by the community's attitudes towards colonization. In order to make the intricately local configurations of this argument clear, this part of the book begins first with the literary and linguistic map of Gujarat.

Linguistic Framework

It is a cliché to begin any discussion of Indian languages by reiterating the polylingual nature of the country. Undeniably, the role of translation in India gains importance from this polylingualism, at the same time, it must be stated that this much-celebrated polylingualism has never been mirrored completely in any systematic effort at translation. The official and commercial discourse of translation in India, from one Indian language into another, or from an Indian language into English, is concerned only with the 'written' and 'recognised' languages. This naturally eliminates a huge range of languages that are considered dialects. For instance, Hindi has official patronage, but Bhojpuri does not figure in any translation scheme because it is a dialect of Hindi, and therefore 'inferior'. Languages seen as 'corrupt' forms (such as Sambhalpuri is of Oriya) remain equally unattended to. Konkani struggled for a long time before it acquired 'recognition'. One of the ways in which some languages gain precedence over others is through a consensus regarding their 'rich' literary traditions. Sumi Krishna asserts that "the belief in the superiority of languages with rich literatures is subtly misplaced. While literature is an important factor in the development of a language, the misconception creeps in when by literature we mean only that which is written" (1991:6). Thus the eighteen odd languages included in the Union today – Assamese, Bengali, Gujarati, Hindi, Kannada, Kashmiri, Konkani (instituted by the Constitution Act, 1992); Malayalam, Manipuri (ins. by the Constitution Act, 1992), Marathi, Nepali (ins. by the Constitution Act, 1992) Oriya, Punjabi, Sanskrit, Sindhi, Tamil, Telugu and Urdu – are fraught with internal hierarchies and competing perceptions. Languages like Hindi and Manipuri, for instance, represent two ends of the linguistic spectrum. The funneling of resources towards education systems, distribution networks and readerships made available to Hindi are not available to Manipuri or Nepali. Languages like Gujarati, Marathi, Malayalam, Tamil, Telugu fall somewhere between the two extremes of the linguistic spectrum (see Devy 1998b). These inequalities get reflected in the activity of translation and consequent 'representation'. For instance, compared to Manipuri and Nepali, Tamil and Malayalam have had more translations for the reason that the former two languages entered the 'official' roster of languages much more recently. The cases of unevenness are many.

The Sahitya Akademi has attempted to correct these inequalities by *aiming* at uniform representation of all 'major' languages, and in recent times, even tribal and oral languages. The General Council laid down the language policy of the Akademi:

> The Akademi will be concerned not only with the languages mentioned in the Indian Constitution but also with other Indian languages, as well as with literary productions in English by Indian nationals. (Rao, 1985:58)

On these grounds the Sahitya Akademi's list of languages also includes marginalized languages such as Maithili, Dogri and more recently Garo and Khasi. Commercial publishers are not accountable for a democratic representation of Indian Literature; hence their choices are confined to the 'major' languages that have a 'market'. The slant of commercial translation activity towards languages like Bengali, Urdu, Kannada and Malayalam is indicative of the 'marketability' of these literatures. The hard fact that a text translated from Dogri, for instance, into any Indian language or English is a marketing risk is sad but undeniable. It is important to de-romanticize the celebration of translation as 'representing' the diversity of India, and to take note of the inequalities that exist in the very act of considering languages.

Coming once again to the question of Gujarati, it passes the test of being a 'major' language by the criteria of the Eighth Schedule as well as the Sahitya Akademi. It is the language of the majority in the state of Gujarat and it also fulfills the following criterion laid down by the Sahitya Akademi:

1. Whether structurally a language is an independent language or is part of a system of a given language
2. Whether it has had a continuous literary tradition and history for at least the last three centuries
3. Whether a sufficiently large number of people use it today as a vehicle of literary and cultural expression
4. Whether it is recognized by the State concerned and/or by some Universities as a medium of instruction and/or as a separate subject of study
5. The number of people using the speech, the current literature that is being produced in it (fiction, essays, other literatures, journals, etc.) may also be considered. (Rao, 1985:59).

Modern Gujarati as spoken and used in literature today is derived from Sanskrit through the intermediate stages of Saurseni Prakrit and Gaurjar Apabrahmsa. Like all the major languages of Northern and Central India, Gujarati belongs to the Indo-Aryan family of languages. During the rule of the Gurjars, (probably a Shaka tribe which entered India in the fifth century A.D and conquered West Rajasthan and most of present-day North Gujarat by the end of the sixth century), the land came to be known as Gurjarata or Gurjar Desha. The term 'Gujarat' had emerged by the tenth century. The first known work written in Gujarati is Hemachandra's *Prakrita Vyakarana* in the eleventh century. The first printed book was completed in the year 1815, after the arrival of printing in Gujarat in 1812. The first Gujarati newspaper, *Mumbai Samachar,* started in 1822 and is the oldest surviving newspaper in the country.

The period of Old Gujarati, beginning from the twelfth century, has many long narrative poems by Jain saint poets. The medieval period (1450- 1850) is a long stretch comprising several historic changes in Gujarati literature. A plethora of poetic forms invented by Narsinh, Akho, Dayaram and Premanand make this period an extremely fertile one. Akha's *chhappas* (terse stanzaic form) are satiric in nature, mocking the blind and polytheistic practices of his time. Mira's love poems also fall into this period; so do Gangasati's songs. Some translation of these Gujarati 'bhakti' poets has been undertaken by different religious trusts, and, more recently, by Sahitya Akademi, New Delhi and the Gujarat Sahitya Akademi. On the whole, the intellectual/radical and literary quality of some of the early poets has been overshadowed by the label of 'devotional poetry'. Audiences outside Gujarat hardly get a flavour (for there has been no equivalent in

Gujarati to A.K. Ramanujan's translations of the vacanas or Dilip Chitre's rendering of Tukaram) of the wit and intellect in some of the poetry of this period.

Narmad and Dalpatram in the nineteenth century begin the 'modern' phase of Gujarati literature. The first Gujarati novel, Nandakisor Mehta's *Karan Ghelo* (1866), and the first social novel, Mahipatram's *Sasu vahu ni ladai* (1866), also belongs to this phase. An interlocking of reformist tendencies and Western genres is the predominant feature of the work of poets exposed to University education in this age. The modern period of Gujarati is extremely complex and indicative of Gujarat's relationship with colonization. The Age of Reformism (*Sudharak Yug*) beginning at the end of the nineteenth century culminates with Gujarati's best-known literary creation, *Saraswati Chandra*. None of the major authors of this period, including Govardhanram Tripathi (the author of *Saraswati Chandra*), is available in English translation.

In the twentieth century, Gujarati literature has been dominated by Gandhi's presence for at least four to five decades. A majority of known authors in Gujarat, up to the nineteen-seventies remain – in acceptance or rejection – influenced by Gandhi. Jhaverchand Meghani, K.M. Munshi, Anantrai Rawal, Ishwarbhai Petlikar, Umashankar Joshi, Dhoomketu, Sundaram and a host of writers belong to the Gandhian phase of Gujarati literature. Compared to the previous period, some of these authors are at least better known, if not read outside Gujarat. With the exception of K.M. Munshi, hardly any author from this period is available in translation. The breakaway from Gandhian thought and the old Sanskritic school of Gujarati literature marks the beginning of another very significant phase of Gujarati literature. Suresh Joshi stands as a colossus in this regard, translated into English for the first time in 1998. Among the established practitioners of Gujarati literature of the contemporary period are Harindra Dave, Chinu Modi, Prabodh Parikh, Rajendra Shah, Niranjan Bhagat, Labhshanker Thaker, Suresh Dalal and many others. In recent times new energies have emerged from the margins of Gujarati literature, mainly from among women and dalits, which seem to draw more attention from translators than mainstream writers of today and yesteryears.

Translation in Gujarat

This section offers an account of translation activity in Gujarat. Although translation from Gujarati into English is of more relevance here, some mention of translations into Gujarati also needs to be made since the latter has had a long and continuous tradition. Translation from Indian as well as European languages has been an integral part of the literary and cultural life of Gujarat. Literary styles in Gujarati literature owe a great deal to translations made available in Gujarati. The difference between what has gone out of Gujarat into other languages (including English) and what has come into the Gujarati language from outside sources is staggering. Surveys undertaken by research students conclude that approximately 1000 works from Indian and some European languages exist in Gujarati translation (see Chaudhuri, 1994). In contrast, very little from Gujarati literature has made inroads into other languages, particularly English, perhaps because English poses its own set of problems and has its own dynamics. The impetus to translate into Gujarati has come mainly from two sources – the establishment of the Gujarat Vernacular Society and Gandhi's emphasis upon translating into the vernaculars. The Gujarat Vernacular Society, the oldest organization of its kind in the state, was established in 1845. A.K. Forbes, with the help of the poet Dalpatram, established this organization to preserve old Gujarati manuscripts and thereby provided a publishing forum for works written in Gujarati. Forbes, who worked for the East India Company and was sent to Ahmedabad as an assistant judge, developed great interest in the history and culture of Gujarat, but found the language unpolished and underdeveloped. Through the activities of the Society, he placed high premium upon translation because that was one of the ways in which he meant to 'improve' the Gujarati language. He remarks:

> When we contribute to a Christian Mission we acknowledge the call. When we try to lift up the language of the province from its present ignoble condition and encourage the more gifted fancies among those to whom it is vernacular, to enlarge, refine and regulate it by manifold application, that it may become a filter to convey from mind to mind and from generation both the beautiful and the true, then too we acknowledge the same call to benefit those among whom for the present we are sojourners. (in Parekh, 1932, I:11)

The relationship between Dalpatram and A.K. Forbes and, through it, the role of the Vernacular Society form a different kind of 'colonial transaction'. The Society, now called the Gujarat Vidya Sabha, is still very active in publishing original works and translation. While it is not within the purview of this study to go into its role in detail, it may be noted that a concerted effort to 'enrich' and 'refine' the Gujarati language found it necessary first to bring translations *into* Gujarati. On the other hand, whenever a language or a culture has been perceived as being rich and dominant, and a repository of ideas, aesthetics and poetics, there has been a rush to translate from it into other 'receptor' languages and cultures. Kapil Kapoor makes an apt comment:

> There is in each act of translation, an attitude towards the source language and a certain assessment of the target language – it is a recognition of the intellectual strength of the source and of a vacuum or gap in the target language/culture. (1997:153)

In the nineteenth century, English texts played the role of 'nurturing', and the 'native' target texts gained 'sustenance'. (A reverse exercise is taking place today, but the implications are not exactly converse. The nuances of this exchange will be dealt with later). The relationship between the English source texts and the Gujarati target texts, was one of reverence and quiet submission on the part of Gujarati. Similar overtones exist even in the Gujarati-Bengali relationship, an issue we briefly revert to later.

Another impetus to translate into Gujarati came from Gandhi's views on translation:

> I consider English as a language for international trade and commerce and therefore, it is necessary that a few people learn it… and I would like to encourage those to be well-versed [in English] and expect them to translate the masterpieces of English into the vernaculars. (in Patel, 1959: 255; *translation mine*)

Gandhi's words form the cornerstone of translation activity in Gujarat. Translation for Gandhi was a process that countered the insularity of cultures; it allowed, to use his own metaphor, the blowing of all winds freely into the house without letting the house get blown away (see Manibhai Patel, 1959). Furthermore, translation into the mother tongue helped in restricting the direct use and dominance of the English language. Interestingly Gandhi's own works were translated by Mahadev Desai very early on. In a fine reversal of events, Gandhi himself translated the *Song Celestial*, Edwin Arnold 's translation of the *Geeta*, into Gujarati so that "every illiterate woman and child in Gujarat should read it" (Gandhi, 1946: Foreword). Mahadev Desai, who wished Gandhi's work to reach a Western audience translated the translation back into the source language, that is English, which itself had been a target language for Edwin Arnold!

It can be concluded from the foregoing that Gujarat has for the longest time accepted the 'donor' status of other languages, especially Sanskrit, English and Bengali. There is a different self-reflexivity about Gujarati literature today that makes the Gujarati literati evaluate translation differently (see Deepak Mehta 1997; Sanchita Guha 1997; V.J. Trivedi 2002). A research study of English writings in Gujarat in the pre-independence era lists ten works translated from Gujarati into English. These include literary and non-literary works, adaptations and free translations (see Joshi, 1992). Of the ten odd works in English translation, translation 'proper' begins only with Mahadev Desai's translations of Gandhi's works in the second and third decades of the twentieth century. Most of the translated works remain unread and unnoticed. They have interested only bibliographers and researchers. In contrast the year 1998-1999 alone witnessed the production of eight English translations from Gujarati, and marked an "an unprecedented event" in terms of quantity and competence (Bhave, 2001:107). A select bibliography of works translated from Gujarati into English in the twentieth century provided at the end of this study points to a dramatic shift in Gujarati translations after 1995. In keeping with the methodology adopted so far, the following discussion provides publishing analyses of the case of Gujarati works in English translation. It is important to remind ourselves of the post-eighties transformation in the English-language publishing industry discussed in the previous chapter and examine the case of Gujarati in that light.

Publishing Analyses

Gujarat has very few institutions engaged in publishing English-language literary works. An exception is the Navjivan Press with its history dating back to Mahatma Gandhi's period in Ahmedabad. The Navjivan Press has for many years published socio-political writings by Gandhi and others coloured by the Gandhian ideology. The Gujarat Sahitya Akademi is the only state run agency with English translations within its purview, its abortive singular attempt at English translation in the eighties notwithstanding.

It may be useful to examine the publication trajectory of English translation from Gujarat in terms of planned and unplanned translation. Planned translation is mainly institutional and is essential to fulfil some constitutional and other obligations. Such translation by the Sahitya Akademi, the National Book Trust and similar agencies is undertaken for integrational purposes and is unconcerned with the demands of society. Jhaverchand Meghani's *Mansai na Deeva* (*Earthen Lamps*, 1979) and Pannalal Patel's *Manvini Bhavai* (*Endurance: A Droll Saga*, 1995) fall under this category. Kundanika Kapadia's *Saat Paglan Aakash maan* (*Seven Steps in the Sky*, 1994) was first published by the Sahitya Akademi, its rights were subsequently bought by Penguin India. This work and the conditions of its publication are a slightly unusual instance of transaction between public and private units in the industry of translation. Presumably it happened in response to the interest in Indian women's texts today. All three works mentioned above were translated under the Sahitya Akademi's scheme of translating award-winning books into as many languages as possible. However, the two works by Jhaverchand Meghani and Pannalal Patel remain somewhat unread and unknown for want of distribution and marketing. It must also be said that of the thirty odd Gujarati literary works which have received the Akademi's awards, from 1955 to the present, less than five have been translated. This shows the discrepancy between the Akademi's expressed policy and its actual implementation. It is also a comment upon the non/availability of translators from Gujarat.

Unplanned translation takes place in many different ways. In some cases, individuals or small presses publish works out of genuine interest and do not always strive to distribute them in the market. The works then remain little known and serve little purpose. C.C. Mehta's play *Aag-gaadi* (*Iron Road*, 1970) and Chandrakant Topiwala's *Contemporary Gujarati Poetry*, 1972 belong to this category. Titles of this nature are added to the list of works translated into English, but make little difference as far as readerships are concerned. Then there are commercial and market-sensitive efforts to publish translations. In this area too Gujarati has fared very badly. Translations of short stories published by Vikas and Jaico were early efforts at 'trade publishing' in the sixties and seventies when the market for English books had not been created. These translations remain unnoticed and languish perhaps in the old records of the publishers concerned. In the current phase of trade publishing, Gujarat appears slowly and steadily in a few translation lists from Macmillan, Oxford University Press, and Kali for Women. Such attempts promise better visibility and distribution and add energy to a latent trend.

It is interesting to view the situation of Gujarati vis-à-vis some of the other 'major' languages in India. The first translation from Malayalam into English, W. Dumergue's rendering of *Indulekha*, was published in 1890. The tradition of translation from Malayalam since then has been in a sense unbroken. Despite the absence of a market, this tradition has made the works of Basheer, M.T. Vasudevan Nair, Narayan Menon available to non- Malayali readers in India and abroad. Bengali had well-known translators such Michael Madhusudan Dutt and R.C. Dutt who had formed a corpus, however small, of works translated into English. By the time Rabindranath Tagore appeared on the Bengali literary scene, there was already a tradition of translating into English. As far as Tamil is concerned, G.U. Pope and others in the nineteenth century had initiated translation by showing interest in the 'wisdom literature' of Tamil. In the present century Ramanujan's translations in the seventies from the Sangam literature have contributed significantly to the knowledge of Tamil literature within and outside India. A wide range of Kannada authors are available in English translation – V.K. Gokak, Shivaram Karanth, Gopalkrishna Adiga, U.R. Ananthamurthy, Girish Karnad, Chandrashekhar Kambar, Anupama Niranjana, Purnachandra Tejaswi and many others. A band of translators from Kannada has been translating and contributing to this body of literature, for example, Ramchandra Sharma, Girish Karnad, A.K. Ramanujan, Tejaswini Niranjana. Marathi too has had some well-known translators such as Dilip Chitre, Gauri Deshpande, Shanta Gokhale and Priya Adarkar. It would be naïve to look for precise equivalence in translated works among all languages. Beyond a point, these comparisons are misleading because of the internal specificities that need to be taken into account. For instance, a fair amount of Assamese poetry has been translated into English. Poets translate each other's work. However, these endeavours, remarks Anjum Hassan, are usually the result of personal interest and rarely recognized as viable or commercial enterprise. According to Hassan, other genres remain more or less untouched because there is never enough of a market, and for languages like Khasi there is no market (1995:26-30). In some cases, the number of works translated into English may not be very large, but a combination of well-known authors, translators and high-profile publishing makes them visible. Extra-literary factors often ensure the circulation and institutionalization of specific texts. Ananthamurthy's *Samskara* was widely discussed and prescribed as a text by universities in India and abroad because Ramanujan translated it and Oxford University Press published it, and Ramanujan's presence in America undoubtedly aided the process of its dissemination. A similar institutionalization took place with Gopinath Mohanty's *Paraja* translated by Bikram Das. As the editor at Oxford University Press indicated, the book figured, through the help of a teacher of Oriya origin, in the syllabus at Cornell University. This ensured readership as well as sales. It has also evoked interest in Oriya among staff and students at Cornell. These stray instances are indicative of apparently accidental circumstances that give prominence to some texts and languages. Gujarati's position vis-à-vis other languages of equal status remains poor in all these respects.

In the last few years, it has become a matter of concern for practitioners and critics of Gujarati literature that some of this literature should reach audiences outside Gujarat. In my interviews with academics, poets and office-bearers concerned with Gujarati literature, it emerged that there was little disagreement about the meagre quantity of Gujarati translated into English, especially when compared with languages like Kannada, Tamil, Malayalam or Bengali (interviews with Bholabhai Patel, Ramlal Parikh and Yashwant Shukla were held in Gujarati, the translations are mine). At the same time, the different explanations throw interesting light on the "marginalization of Gujarati literature in the national consciousness" (Ramanathan and Kothari, 1998: xvii).

It may be worth exploring whether this 'underestimation' is the cause or the effect of translation, for instance, Bholabhai Patel notes that there has been an apathy towards Gujarati literature. Those who know Gujarati, he adds, know little English and those competent in English are indifferent to Gujarati literature (1989, 1-5). Ramlal Parikh, the vice-chancellor of the Gujarat Vidyapeeth, on the other hand, feels that Gujarat has not developed a "science of translation. It has focused upon transcreation or adaptations" (personal interview, 1997; all subsequent references are to this interview). At the same time, he maintains that the Gujarati diaspora in Western countries has become self-aware about the Gujarati culture and literature, and will play an important role in the future. If Bholabhai Patel thinks that there has been apathy on the part of Gujaratis, Yashwant Shukla (a well-known critic and eminent man of letters) feels that it does not "become" the locals of Gujarat to translate themselves. The demand for translation has to come from outside agencies. Shukla feels that "things like these have to flower on their own. Systems have to evolve for translation and then individuals will do it". Patel's point of view differs from this and he draws attention to the parallel growth of Kannada and Gujarati up to the beginning of this century. Kannada literature is known within and outside India through the availability of a wide range of authors. This is because Kannada generated a group of English teachers who also wrote in their mother tongues, and this helped them maintain a literary relationship with both languages. K. Satchidnandan, the secretary of the Sahitya Akademi, Delhi voices the same point of view by saying that in Kerala, English teachers have maintained an organic relationship with their mother-tongue and that has helped the cause of translation. This means that English teachers constitute a large segment of translators' communities everywhere. It also implies that inadequate dialogue between departments of English and Indian literature undermines possibilities of translation. One of the ways in which some languages found their way into English earlier than others is through the assertion of literary communities. Satchidanandan remarks that "certain languages have been assertive and successfully propagated their literatures and somehow captured the attention" (personal interview). The lack of effort on the part of the Gujaratis to propagate Gujarati work outside Gujarat may be termed 'apathy'; or it may also be as modesty and self-effacement.

A common premise running through all the arguments made by those in Gujarat and those outside about Gujarat's lack of 'representation' is that Gujarat does not have many bilingual persons who have a simultaneous and equal command over Gujarati and English. The authorities at the Sahitya Akademi and Katha admitted having had difficulty in finding good translators from Gujarat. Parikh noted that:

> Gujaratis being in business needed the local language and not English. Therefore, they have not had a very deep interaction with English. As for professionals, they carried their careers abroad, so the state is not left with many people with a mastery in both languages.

Patel attributes the lack of bilinguals largely to Gujarat's language policy, which systematically undermined English and created two generations after independence with poor levels of competence in English. Shukla tends to believe that the impact of the language policy on this matter is not a crucial factor. However, compared to some other states, Gujarat did not have close contact with the British. It is clear that there has obviously not been a concerted effort to make Gujarati literature known outside Gujarat. According to G.N. Devy, the Gujaratis are, by and large, indifferent to translation. Gujarat has never been dominated emotionally by the West (personal interview, 1997). Translation into English then is the product of a much more complex set of circumstances than is generally acknowledged. The following section explores the socio-historical conditions for translation in Gujarati in the colonial and postcolonial contexts.

Socio-historical Background

Gujarat's first contact with the British took place as early as 1613 when the British opened their first trade centre in Surat. This was later shifted to Bombay. In the following years with the decline of the central Mughal authority Gujarat was plagued by gradual cultural decay and a number of small princely states emerged. Recurrent raids by the Marathas to extract revenue compounded the feeling of insecurity. In 1803, the East India Company acquired possession of the leading city of Broach; and the Company's victory at the Battle of Kirkee in 1818 stabilized English rule in Gujarat. After a long period of political unrest and chaos, Gujarat once again felt a sense of security and peace. By the second decade of the nineteenth century, Gujarat was completely under colonial rule and that status remained 'unchallenged' till the end of the First World War in 1918. Gujarat also remained relatively indifferent to the First War of Independence in

1857. But outlining these events in such broad strokes falsifies the mixed quality of Gujarat's response to colonialism. Colonialism was not challenged militantly and politically till Gandhi appeared on the scene. However, in the areas of economics and commerce, moral and social issues, and more importantly, English education, Gujarati intellectuals and poets displayed an interesting range of responses. Among early responses to colonialism, Gujarat's first modern poet, Narmad, read an essay in Surat on the value of forming co-operatives and associations. Dalpatram in the same year, that is 1851, read a poem on the invasion of mechanized industry through the West and exhorted people to adopt industrialization.

The same practical and business-like approach governed Gujarat's attitude to education. In 1835, with the passing of Macaulay's (in) famous Educational Minute, educational policies for all the states had to be shaped. States were free to accept or to modify the new educational system, and some did modify much to the chagrin of the English government. Mountstart Elphinstone, then governor of Bombay (Gujarat in the pre-independence era figured in the Northern Presidency), followed a policy of non-interference in this matter, and native schools teaching through Marathi and Gujarati were left alone. In Ahmedabad and Surat too, the efforts of schools teaching English received a lukewarm response. When the authorities of the Bohras' College at Surat were asked to arrange for English teaching at government expense, they politely declined the offer, saying: "within the College no other study is permitted, but what is contained in the books of religion" (Chavda, n.d, 247). In another instance, a petition to establish an English school in Ahmedabad was made. Interestingly enough, the petitioners were all Marathi-speaking persons and professed to speak on behalf of the inhabitants of Ahmedabad. The Bombay Native Education Society, which also catered to the educational needs of schools of indigenous learning, was gradually replaced by schools based on the western model, in Gujarat and Maharashtra. A continuous increase in the number of vernacular schools and pupils attending them testified to the fact that the Western type of education through the vernacular evoked a very positive response from the people. The controversy between the Anglicists and Classicists in Bengal found a resolution in education through the mother tongue in the bilingual state of Maharashtra.

Considering the fact that the Gujarati intellectual's response to English literature was very enthusiastic, this restricted use of English is puzzling. For instance, after the consolidation of Bombay University in 1857, the first two generations of Gujarati writers – Narmad, Navalram, Ramanbhai Neelkanth, Manibhai, Govardhanram Tripathi and Anandshankar – were all beneficiaries of English education, and drunk with the nectar of English poetry. Narsimhrao's *Kusummala* (1887) conceived along the lines of Palgrave's *Golden Treasury* represented the domination of the Romantic style of poetry for many years. The tradition of writing English prefaces was evident in the first political novel of Gujarat, *Karan Ghelo* or *The last Rajput King*; the first social novel, *Sasuvahu ni Ladai*, the travelogue *Hind ane Britannia*, and much later Govardhanram's

Saraswati Chandra indicate the use and acceptance of English. At the same time, most of the writing in English was closely intertwined with agendas of reformism, and was hardly ever a literary exercise for its own sake. For instance, Mahipatram wrote an English preface to his novel and 'explained' his choice:

> Believing that an appeal, through the English Language to such of my enlightened countrymen as can understand it, on the crying social evils exposed in this book, will be more effective for their removal, and for rousing the sympathy of the educators and civilisers of this country. ((1866) 1996:7)

Writing prefaces in English, Gujarati novels and travelogues clearly mapped out the boundaries of English and the mother tongue.

We now turn to Gujarat's economic situation and awareness in the nineteenth century. Gujarat had, very early on, woken up to the fact of economic exploitation under colonial rule. The Gujarat Vernacular Society published translations of economic treatises written in other languages and Gujarati writers like Navalram and Hargovindas discussed the theme of economic exploitation under colonial rule from 1870 onwards. Kantawala openly spoke of *swadeshi* and *swadesh prem*. The fact is that Gujarat had a self-sufficient economy that required little intervention through a Western type of education. The predominance of trade and of the mercantile class and the existence of about 200 feudal states in the region did not call for a high economic investment in English-related jobs. Secondly, the enterprising nature of the Gujaratis made people evolve their own means of economic progress. The market for cotton-trade and the cotton and other ancillary industries that burgeoned towards the close of the nineteenth century comprise another framework for assessing the relative insignificance of English. The response of the city of Ahmedabad to the commercial challenge of British rule is especially revealing. Its textiles competed very well with European rivals in the international market, and with the exception of a handful rich *seths* who took to Anglicised ways for a brief period at the end of the nineteenth century; the city showed little desire to emulate the West. According to Sunil Khilnani, Ahmedabad industrialized itself under its own steam, through its own language without noticeable British investment, and with little disturbance to its existing cultural habits (1997:113). Thus a peculiar brand of nationalism, to be defined not in terms of patriotism but a civic society, enabled Gujarat to face challenges from the West in a unique manner, and prepared the ground for Gandhi.

Gandhi's presence in Gujarat in the first four or five decades of the twentieth century reinforced the need for a self-sufficient economy and education. The ideological commitments of institutions like the Gujarat Vidyapeeth and the Navjeevan Press reflect a longstanding native tradition that has not easily allowed the foundations to be shaken. Concrete testimonies of this lie in schools, universities, gram vidyapeeths and the entrenched tradition of co-operatives.

Gandhi's influence in matters of culture and education are of very direct concern to us here since they have shaped Gujarat's language policy to a large degree. Other factors contributing to this phenomenon are related to Gujarat's political intervention in matters of education; its identity as a state separate from Maharashtra, and the legacies of its relationship with British rule. The culmination of all this was a strong resistance to English in post-independence India. It has finally led to the 'great debate' about the English language.

Language Policy

After the 1920s, the Mahatma was a governing force in all social reform and educational issues. His impact upon education is of very direct relevance because of the fact that, along with many other unconscious legacies of the colonial rule, it determined the location of English in postcolonial Gujarat. He announced in the *Young India* of 1928: "Among the many evils of foreign rule this blighting imposition of a foreign medium upon the youth of the country will be counted by history as one of the greatest". Gandhi believed that education through English was "unnecessarily expensive", and that it "prevented the growth of our vernaculars" (1953:59). He also believed that for the first seven years of schooling, it was very burdensome for a child to be learning through a foreign medium; the medium of instruction in those years should therefore be only the mother-tongue. These views of Gandhi regarding English language and education found unquestioning support among a huge section of Gujaratis, some of whom were policy makers in matters of education. The placement of English in Gujarat since then has been fraught with severe differences and conflicts.

After independence, the question of the language for administration and education had to be resolved at both the national and state levels. Education was a subject on the state list and the debate about the medium of instruction in primary, secondary schools and in higher education took on a different hue and shade in every state. When India became independent, and the medium of instruction in schools and universities had to be decided at the state level, the stand taken by many in Gujarat proceeded from the Gandhian philosophy of education. Maganbhai Desai (1964:9), the Registrar of the Gujarat Vidyapeeth, interpreted the Centre's desire to retain English as "vested interests which continue to dominate us even today". He stated the following tenets for education in an independent nation-state:

1. English should have no place whatsoever in the curriculum of the first seven years (i.e. from standard first to standard seventh.) From the fifth standard the study of the national language should begin.
2. From standards 8th to 11th, i.e. during the four years of High School, English should be introduced. It need not be compulsory. Those not taking up English may take up, besides the mother tongue, any one of the

Indian languages. The more we live in Swaraj the more we feel the need
of knowing Indian languages other than our mother tongues.

There was, by and large, agreement all over the country that primary and secondary education had to be re-grouped as seven years of primary and four years
of secondary education. Earlier on it was four years of primary and seven years
of secondary. A contentious issue in Gujarat was the 'proper place' of English
in the curriculum. This apparently small matter assumed huge proportions as
letters and articles proclaiming the ideological implications of each stand were
discussed in public. It was a long drawn out debate – from about 1945 to the
early 1970s – its intensity reminiscent of the controversy between the Classicists and Anglicists in the nineteenth century India. The two divergent groups,
which we shall, for convenience's sake, call the 'Gujarati lobby' and the 'English lobby', stood for introducing English from standard VIII and from standard
V, respectively. It is crucial to note that there was no conflict between the two
groups as far as the basic medium of instruction was concerned. (The Gujarati
Press, in a facetious vein, referred to the two groups as *Thakore Panch* and
Thakore Aath because the champions on the two sides bore the names of
Thakorebhai Desai and Thakorebhai Thakor, respectively). Even a staunch sup-
porter from the "English lobby", Niranjan Bhagat maintains that it is "sinful" to
think of education in a language other than the mother tongue. However, Bhagat
has strong differences with what he calls, the "pseudo-Gandhians" regarding
the position of English in the curriculum. In addition to introducing English
from the fifth standard, his group also advocated making it a compulsory subject thereafter (Bhagat, 1974). The 'Gujarati lobby', on the other hand, said that
English should be made optional in secondary schools. This was because many
students performed poorly at the Matriculation examination owing to their inability to deal with English. Since many members of the Gujarati lobby occupied
key positions in the University and its affiliated institutions, the language policy
conceived by them, though hotly contested, came into force. This controversy
also needs to be seen in the light of Gujarat's formation as a separate state.
Before 1960 Gujarat was a part of the Bombay Presidency and the new state,
formed on the basis of language, obviously needed to privilege its language to
reinforce its identity. Consequently there was a stronger drive to switch over to
Gujarati at all levels.

   The debate regarding English at the school level continued unabated as the
years went by. The supporters of English increased, to some extent, because the
issue of the "official language" remained undecided even at the national level.
Yet another development is related to the Gujarat University. Kakasaheb Kalelkar
stated the question: "When can we call this university the Gujarat University?"
and gave the answer: "When the medium of its instruction and examinations is
Gujarati" (in Chavda, 258). On 13th September 1960, it was announced in the
Vidhan Sabha (the state Legislative Assembly) that the Government desired to
amend the relevant statute of the University, by which from November 1960,

the medium of instruction in the Gujarat University would be Gujarati only. With this, colleges affiliated to Gujarat University could not teach English and the examinations were to be held in the regional language. A non-Gujarati resident of Ahmedabad, Mr. Mudholkar secured from the Gujarat High Court a decision that the Legislative Assembly had no authority to determine any medium of instruction for Universities since this was within the University's own jurisdiction.

As things stand now, English in local and municipal schools is taught from the fifth standard as an optional subject. It is compulsory in standards VIII and IX. Again in standard X, it is optional, and the fear of failing the Board examination makes many students drop English because it is optional. Those who do not offer English in the tenth standard naturally avoid it in the twelfth. As a result most metropolitan and mofussil undergraduate colleges affiliated to Gujarat University have students with very little (as little as two years) English. They are referred to as "B Stream" students, and the syllabus prescribed for them is different from the syllabus for those who have studied English in the tenth and twelfth standards. Thus a systematic undermining of English at various levels, a consequence of Gujarat's language policy, has led to very low levels of English.

According to a research study, the evolution of an education system in a given region is often influenced by the socio-cultural background of the community which is its clientele, whose aspirations and limitations it caters to (Rangarajan, 1986:15). Gujarat's long history of a business culture and a value system dominated by a commercial outlook seem to have undermined the goals of education. A Gujarati with his keen business acumen takes a cost-benefit approach to education; the "making of the mind" counts for little on the whole. The study, which was carried out by T. Rangarajan with a view to finding out why students from Gujarat do not apply for or are not successful at all-India competitive examinations, says this about the state:

1. Gujarat has a long tradition and cultural life that never came into direct contact with the British. It had a large number of native states, and only Ahmedabad and Kheda were under British rule. Englishness did not permeate deeply into the lives of the people.
2. A whole urban and petty bourgeoisie emerged as a result of the British system of education in other parts of India. That never happened in Gujarat. Traditionally there was no professional class. There were only mill owners and businessmen. They did not require the British education for furthering their economic prospects nor they did need public services. The educated Gujaratis that did take up professional careers opted for business-connected courses.

Gujarat Today

While the factors outlined above have led to a situation in which Gujarat compares unfavourably with other states in the matter of competence in English, we need also to take account of other factors which point in a different direction, thanks to the far-sightedness of a few families or individuals. Gujarat has marginalized itself educationally from the national mainstream through its language policy. But the fact is that it is the location of some of the most prestigious educational centres in the whole country. The Indian Institute of Management, the National Institute of Design, the BM Institute of Mental Health, the Centre for Environmental Planning and Technology, and most recently, the National Institute of Fashion Technology – are all premier educational institutes, entry to which is highly competitive on a national scale. We need to ask three questions:

(1) How did these extremely modern institutions come into existence here, given the non-Western bias of the state?
(2) What relationship have they with society at large in the state?
(3) Can they act as vehicles of English carrying the language into, and out of Gujarat (an important consideration for translation projects in Gujarat)?

A handful of wealthy industrialists in Ahmedabad, most notably the Lalbhai and Sarabhai families, were very conscious of the importance of education. The Sarabhais as a family were unusual for Gujarat inasmuch as they combined a great admiration for Western education with nationalist sympathies (rather like the Nehrus). The sons were all educated either at Oxford or Cambridge and on their return to India, set up institutes to bring the best from abroad to Ahmedabad! Vikram Sarabhai, a scientist, set up the Physical Research Laboratory, the Indian Institute of Management, the Ahmedabad Textile Industry's Research Association and the Community Science Centre. His brother set up the National Institute of Design and the BM Institute of Mental Health. These institutes which attracted students, scientists, research scholars from all parts of the country, created a culture which was distinctly non-Gujarati and used the medium of English.

However, the irony is that few Gujaratis have been able to gain entry into these institutions and the reason for this must be attributed, at least partly, to their poor levels of English. The institutes thus stand as islands of excellence, cut off from the surrounding flow of the city, participating hardly at all in its cultural life and housing largely non-Gujaratis. However, one may infer that there has been, over a period of 30-40 years, a trickle-down cultural effect from these places into society at large. At the very least, their presence and prestige have served as reminders of an inheritance thrown away and now to be recovered and that English is indispensable for the operation of recovery.

The third question was related to the role these institutes may play in disseminating a cosmopolitan culture in the state. As awareness of the globalizing process gets underway, one finds that increasingly, students from the city's colleges are attempting to enter these places at least as trainees. A place like the National Institute of Design, which takes in about 30-40 students from all over India every year, promotes a very modernist culture, into which a fraction of

Gujarat's students may be absorbed. Cultural events like the garba organized by and for institutes like the NID or CEPT bring hordes of local people onto the campus and give them a taste of something different. Research institutes like the PRL and the Institute of Plasma Research have taken to Open House Days during which the public is allowed access to the premises and given information regarding the work done there. From these events (of fairly recent origin) one may infer that interactions between elitist institutes and the general public is steadily increasing. The implication for English is that such sustained exposure, may lead to an increased demand for English language skills which may enable the locals to compete favourably for entry into the prestigious educational and research institutes in their midst.

We have noted above that the trajectory of educational and research institutes in Ahmedabad has very gradually had an effect on the people's consciousness in the state. It needs to be emphasized that, like elite centres anywhere in the country, these institutions run entirely in English. This has served as one contributory factor to offset the negative attitude towards and neglect of English. Furthermore, the hold of the makers of the old language policy has begun to wear off with time, and the new classes forming in post-colonial Gujarat have not inherited the baggage of antipathy towards English. The close ties that Gujarat had had with English in the time of Nanalal, Kant and Govardhanram snapped after the third decade of the twentieth century when Gujarat was wholly involved in the Freedom Movement. The language policy which rested on a rejection of colonialism was responsible for at least two generations who used hardly any English for purposes of communication. A literary relationship with the English language that might have fostered writing in English or translating into it was out of the question.[1]

However, trends in Gujarat today seem to express a desire for a re-alliance with the English language. This is likely to have a tremendous impact upon translation. Before we turn to translation itself, let us first read the signs of our time.

Gujarat in the last decade, especially after India's drive towards 'liberalization' and an 'open economy' is a changed place. Although my observations apply to large cities like Ahmedabad and Surat, the change is likely to have percolated to smaller towns as well. First of all, there is a re-shaping and re-definition of Gujarat's attitudes to English. There are signs of an English-reading public today – as testified to by at least three new bookshops, and the establishment of the newspaper *The Asian Age*. The emergence of a middle class, which can spend money on books and send its children to English medium schools, has changed the face of the reading public in Ahmedabad. Earlier, the reading

---

[*] D.F. Karaka's weekly comic column *"Arre Bhai, shun chhe?"* in *Current* all through the 50s and 60s showed two Gujaratis in Gandhi caps, exchanging views in very broken English – and every column had "Boycott British Language" as a closing rubric. This was clearly a sarcastic allusion to the Boycott British Goods campaign started by Gandhi.

of English books was confined to a very small section of teachers and intellectuals who constituted the only clientele of old shops such as Sastu Kitab Ghar and the New Order Book Company. The activity of reading in English was relatively low-profile and English did not form a part of all private and public spaces. On the other hand, the opening of a large bookstore like Crossword today is a clear sign of change in readership patterns in Gujarat. Although some part of its clientele today consists of non-Gujarati professionals, a very large proportion of sales is accounted for by middle-class Gujaratis buying English books for their children. Gaurav Shah (owner, Crossword) asserts that children's books in English sell the most (personal interview 15 January 1999). For a new middle class anxious to give its children a competitive edge in a global future, English is seen to be indispensable.

If these are manifestations of the 'presence' of English, there are also attempts to make it available to all sections. Various sociological and economic changes have created a need for English in the state. The shift from the tradition of 'family businesses' to salaried jobs and professions is one reason for this new demand for English. This shift obviously does not apply to all classes and Gujarat is still a 'business-oriented' state; however, interaction even in business, is not confined to the state alone. More and more people do business with other states and abroad as well as through exports. Thus opportunities for using English have proliferated in a state that did not, for a long time, feel that English was required for economic advancement. Also, huge numbers of people from the weaker sections, i.e. castes and classes which have never had the privilege of education, are now being educated. The democratization of education creates a desire to use this education by entering professions. There has also been a concurrent movement from villages to cities, reinforcing the need to know English. For a very long time, jobs as operators and receptionists in good companies were the prerogative of non-Gujaratis, since they always had better English. Increasingly local people are competing for these jobs with outsiders. In such a situation English becomes a crucial means of climbing the occupational ladder.

Another impetus for learning English comes from the desire to go abroad. The Gujarati community is perhaps the largest constituency among South Asian immigrants in the United States. English now becomes absolutely essential, and since the schools do not impart intensive learning, other avenues are sought and found. English coaching classes which 'supplement' English outside school hours and prepare those going abroad with communication skills in English, abound today in the state. The mushrooming of English speaking classes can be seen not only in big cities like Ahmedabad and Surat, but also in the 'mofussil' parts of Gujarat. Thus market demand and the norms of professionalism have made the middle class Gujarati aware of the 'importance' of English.

Coming back to the migrant population, its impact is felt in several ways. The monetary remittances of this constituency change the economy of the home state (a fact not peculiar to Gujarat alone); and influence the cultural make-up of family members living in the home state. At the same time, it also constitutes an important market to which the resident Gujaratis supply products, especially 'cultural' products. Manifestations of this take the form of certain kinds of print and visual media (literature and mythology through books and video cassettes) made available to the NRIs in English in response to their nostalgia for 'home'. For instance, there is an industry concerned with translating Gujarati songs and stories into English for non-resident children who can obtain access to 'Gujarati culture' through English and whose parents wish to provide them with some sense of 'roots'. The 'poor' distribution and 'negligible' sales of Meghani's book *Earthen Lamps* was mentioned in an earlier section. According to the owner of a local bookshop, the book was somewhat more successful with the emigrant Gujaratis who wanted their children and friends to read the great classic. For those with no Gujarati, this was possible only through an English translation.

Apart from the literary and educational shifts just outlined, Gujarat has also emerged as the one of the most urbanized states in the country, second only to Maharashtra. Although its standards of education may not compare with those of Kerala, Tamil Nadu, Karnataka, or Maharashtra, it has emerged as a very important centre in India's newly liberalized and open economy and attracted investors from outside the state and the country. It is the location of some of the leading petrochemical and pharmaceutical industries on the subcontinent. With so many changes, a new consumerist middle class has come into being. This class is not deeply involved with the civic life of the state but it responds to the global demands of individual progress through education and aggressive drive. As Gujarat catches up with the new capitalistic ethos of India today and seeks to take its place in the global market, it readjusts its position regarding English.

It is clear from the foregoing that English is gaining in importance for reasons both commercial and non-materialistic. One aspect of the state's multi-pronged effort to take the lead is the desire and need to project the richness of its cultural heritage. Harish Khare aptly comments: "The choice before the state is to find an optimum mix of its national heritage, the globalizing instincts of its international connections (the overseas Gujaratis), and its regional pride" (1998:23). The dance festivals in Modhera, and the development of the Rani-Vav at Patan are visible signs of this thrust. At a less noticeable level, centres devoted to Gujarati literature are steadily focusing on translation activity. The first Sahitya Akademi (Western Zone) Translation Workshop was held in Ahmedabad in 1996 in which Gujarati poems were translated into the Indian languages of the Western zone *and* into English The Gujarat Sahitya Akademi has recently revived its defunct translation programme mentioned earlier. Since the year 2000, it has published at least five translations in English a year. In almost all cases, the translators hail from the English academia of the state. The Gujarat Sahitya Parishad has now embarked on an ambitious translation project focused upon the best of old, medieval, and modern Gujarati literature. The Parishad's translation project was set in motion in 1999 under the chairmanship of Niranjan Bhagat (a reputed Gujarati poet and a teacher of English). Once again, the Parishad has managed to garner most support for this project from English lecturers in the city of Ahmedabad. In the year 2000, the Gujarat Sahitya Akademi conducted its first workshop on English translations of Gujarati short stories and an anthology, produced as an outcome of this workshop, is due for publication. In the meanwhile, a band of intellectuals from Gujarat (Chinu Modi, a writer, R.A. Dave, an ex-English teacher, VJ. Trivedi, an ex-English teacher) started a Translation Trust in 2002. The Trust has been formed through funds gathered from well-to-do industrialists as well as Gujarat's most popular spiritual leader Morari Baapu! Since state-run establishments like the Parishad and the Gujarat Akademi confine themselves to 'mainstream' Gujarati writing, representation of marginalized literatures has willy-nilly fallen under the purview of alternative institutions such as the recently formed Dalit Sabha and Dalit Sahitya Akademi. The Dalit institutions are formed exclusively for providing encouragement and expression to literature produced by groups suffering from caste-discrimination. The Bibliography shows two volumes of Dalit poetry and Dalit short stories translated into English by English teachers Darshana Trivedi and Rupalee Burke and published by the Dalit Sahitya Akademi. The list also includes mention of the first Dalit novel translated by Rita Kothari and due for publication by the Oxford University Press. Texts from marginalized sections stand better chances of translation and publication now and English teachers play an active role in these developments. It is clear in a period of five short years the repercussions of economic, social and cultural change have made themselves felt and translation activity is one such. Translation in these new circumstances has chances of not just surviving, but also of acquiring desirability. If translation 'promotes' a regional text (thereby addressing the need for regional pride), it also joins hands with the project of 'Indian Literature' (symptomatic of the need for 'pan-Indian' images) and simultaneously it makes homegrown products available in a language that everybody, including the overseas Gujaratis, understands.

Gujarati Works in English Translation: A Bibliographical Supplement

I have presented below some bibliographical information. It does not aim at being a comprehensive bibliography of works translated from Gujarati into English. Poems and short stories from Gujarati have appeared in some distinguished anthologies and journals.* However the exercise of locating each and every poem or a short story was not directly relevant to thrust of "The case of Gujarati" to

---

*See Susie Tharu and K. Lalitha eds. *Women Writing in India* 2 vols. (New Delhi: Oxford University Press, 1993); Arlene Zaide ed. *Women's Voices* (Penguin India, 1992) and Vinay Dharwadker and A.K. Ramanujan eds. *Modern Indian Poetry* (New Delhi: Oxford Univerity Press, 1994). The series of Katha Prize Stories carries, annually, short stories from many Indian languages including Gujarati.

which this section forms a supplement. I have therefore restricted to works published in a book form and belonging to the twentieth century. *

Translations from Gujarati into English

Poetry *

Contemporary Gujarati Poetry, trans. Chandrakant Topiwala (Surat: Western India Publishing Company, 1972)

Devotional Songs from Gujarat, trans. and ed. Dahyabhai Patel (Ahmedabad: Gurjar Grantha Bhavan Trust, 1981)

Devotional Songs of Narsi Mehta, trans. Swami Mahadevananda (Delhi: Motilal Banarsidas, 1985)

Sunrise on Snow Peaks: Haiku of Sneharashmi, trans. by the poet, (Gandhinagar: Gujarat Sahitya Akademi, 1986)

Love Poems and Lyrics from Gujarat, (Gujarat: Gurjar Grantha Ratna Karyalaya, 1987)

Vibrations: Poems of Suresh Dalal, trans. by the poet and others (Bombay: Strand Book Stall, 1989)

Wings of the Soul: Poems of Akha, trans. Krishnaditya (Berkeley: Asian Humanities Press, 1992)

Modern Gujarati Poetry: A Selection, trans. Suguna Ramanathan and Rita Kothari, (New Delhi: Sahitya Akademi, 1998)

Eklavyas with Thumbs: Selections from Gujarati Dalit Literature, trans. K.M. Sheriff (Pushpam, Ahmedabad, 1999)

Selected Poems of Umashankar Joshi, trans. Dushyant Pandya (Gujarat Sahitya Akademi, 2000)

The Silver Lining: Dalit poetry in English, trans. Rupalee Burke and Darshana Trivedi (Gujarat Dalit Sahitya Akademi 2000)

Selected Poems of Dhanvanti, trans. Dhanvanti (Gujarat Sahitya Akademi, 2001)

Celebration of Divinity: Poems of Narsinh Mehta, trans. Darshana Trivedi (Gujarat Sahitya Akademi, 2001)

Coral Island: Prawal Dweep, by Niranjan Bhagat, trans. Suguna Ramanathan, and Rita Kothari (Gujarat Sahitya Akademi, forthcoming)

---

*Special numbers of *Mahfil* IX:1 (1973) and the *Journal of South Asian Literature* (Spring 1973) carry poems of Umashankar Joshi. Anthologies of Indian Poetry published by the Indian Council of Cultural Relations and the Sahitya Akademi aiming at a 'democratic' representation, include Gujarati Poetry. Also see Medieval Indian Literature: An Anthology ed. Ayyappa Panikker (Sahitya Akademi, New Delhi, 1999).

*For a list of works translated from Gujarati into English in the nineteenth century and some part of the twentieth century, see Jatindra Mohan Mohany, *Indian Literature in English: A Bibliography* (Central Institute of Indian Languages, 1984) and Yashodhan Joshi, *The English Writings in Gujarat 1750-1850,* unpublished dissertation (Gujarat University, 1992).

Fiction

Selected stories from Gujarat, trans. Sarla Jagmohan (Bombay: Jaico Publishing House, 1961 rpt. 2001)

K. M. Munshi, *Jaya Somnath,* (novel), trans. H.M. Patel (Bharatiya Vidya Bhawan, 1976, rpt.1988) Mumbai

Jhaverchand Meghani, *An Earthen Lamp*, trans. Vinod Meghani (New Delhi: Sahitya Akademi, 1979)

Gujarati short stories: An Anthology, ed. and intro. Sarla Jagmohan (New Delhi: Vikas Publishing House, 1982)

Chandrakant Bakshi, *Lost Illusions,* trans. Sarla Jagmohan (New Delhi: Sterling Publishers, 1989)

Kundanika Kapadia, *Seven Steps to the Sky*, trans. Kunjbala and William Anthony (Delhi: Penguin India, 1994)

Harindra Dave, *Henceforth*, trans. Bharti Dave (Madras: Macmillan India, 1995)

Pannalal Patel, *Endurance: A Droll Saga*, trans. V.Y. Kantak (New Delhi: Sahitya Akademi, 1995)

K. M. Munshi, *The Master of Gujarat*, trans. N.D. Jotwani (Bharatiya Vidya Bhawan, 1995)

Kanji Patel, *The Rear Verandah*, trans. Nikhil Khandekar. (Madras: Macmillan India, 1998)

Suresh Joshi, *The Crumpled Letter,* trans. Tridip Suhrud (Madras: Macmillan India, 1998)

Vinod Meghani, *Oceanside Blues*, trans. Dhruv Bhatt, Sahitya Akademi, New Delhi, 1999)

Tongues of Fire: Dalit stories in English, trans. Darshana Trivedi and Rupalee Burke (Gujarat Dalit Sahitya Akademi 2000)

Bhupen Khakhar, trans. G.N. Devy, Naushil Mehta, Bina Srinivasan (Katha, New Delhi) 2001.

New Horizons in Women's Writing: Stories by Gujarati Women, trans. Ameena Amin and Manju Verma, (Gujarat Sahitya Akademi, 2002)

Modern Gujarati Short Story, ed. Bholabhai Patel, (Gujarat Sahitya Akademi, forthcoming)

Stories of Suresh Joshi, translated and ed. Birje Patil (Sahitya Akademi, New Delhi)

Worlds of fiction by Gujarati Women, trans. Rita Kothari (Kali for Women, forthcoming)

Angaliyat: The Stepchild, trans. Rita Kothari (Oxford University Press, forthcoming)

Drama

C.C. Mehta, *Iron Road,* trans. by the author (Bombay: Thacker and Company Ltd., 1970)

Shiv Kumar Joshi, *He Never Slept so Long*, trans. by the author (Calcutta: Writers' Workshop, 1972)

Jayana Sheth, *K.M. Munshi: A sculptor: A Critical study of K.M. Munshi,* (Bombay:

Bhartiya Vidya Bhawan, 1979) This study includes the complete translation of Munshi's play *Dhruvasvaminidevi*, trans. Jayana Sheth.

Madhu Rye, *Tell me the Name of a Flower and The Terrace,* trans. Vijay Padaki (Seagull Publications: Calcutta, 2000)

Non-Fiction

M. K. Gandhi, *My Experiments with Truth,* trans. Mahadev Desai (Ahmedabad: Navjivan Press, 1927)

M. K. Gandhi, *Satyagraha in South Africa,* trans. Mahadev Desai (Ahmedabad: Navjivan Press, 1928)

------ *Collected Works,* (Publications Division, Ministry of Information & Broadcasting, Government of India, 1958)

Essays of Suresh Joshi, trans. V.Y. Kantak (Sahitya Akademi, New Delhi)

8.   Summing Up

As I conclude the last chapter of *Translating India* on a note of optimism for Gujarat's new openness to English translation, the state itself is embroiled in the worst-ever communal violence. Judging by externals alone, it is not possible to see any incongruence because a cultural/intellectual/literary activity such as translation and Gujarat's increasingly fundamentalist outlook, laid bare after February 2002, have really no connection at the moment. However, *Translating India* has consistently maintained a stand that literary and para-literary forces do interact in big and small ways although the effects are not always visible for theorization in the present. Translation scholars and social-literary historians may have to wait and see what implications the Gujarat of this moment has for literary activities in future. Would state-sponsored institutions like the Sahitya Parishad and the Gujarat Sahitya Akademi monitor the selection of texts to suit the dominant point of view? Would a strengthening of narrow religious and linguistic outlooks determine the ethnicity of authors or translators or even the content of texts? The previous chapter outlined the trajectory of Gujarat's relationship with English in terms of its shift from hostile indifference to an urgent acceptance manifest in the roaring business of English coaching classes, among other things. While the shift is ungainsayable, it co-exists with residual prejudices against English, again made more pronounced during the state's perception of the media coverage of the recent riots. Reacting to the English visual and print media's scathing criticism of the establishment's complicity in the violence, the state denounced the "English educated, convent-bred journalists" who 'maligned' the reputation of Gujarat (See *Vishwa Hindu Samachar*, April 2002). The view found supporters in a large majority of the Gujarati readers, equally suspicious of outsiders who write in English. At the same time, even as I write this, there are more signs of English as well as translation expansion. These tensions and contradictions may perhaps add further dimensions to the story of English translation in Gujarat, the effects of which we can only speculate and not conclude. The questions raised here underscore the possibilities of different ways of telling the story in future.

In fact as we turn from the essay on Gujarat and go back to the previous essays in this study, there appear a host of issues that serve as topics for research scholars. In an attempt to capture a flux, *Translating India* fixed (or rather restricted) its gaze upon the present moment, so that even the historical inquiry in "Recalling: Translations in colonial India" began with printing and translation in the nineteenth century. Undoubtedly, the origins of English translation lie in the contexts of the late eighteenth and the nineteenth century. However, a historical inquiry of translation could also extend in time to Sanskrit-to-Indian languages translations before the nineteenth century and in space to include Indological translations by German scholars to examine different antecedents, perhaps. The story of translations from N.B. Halhed to Rabindranath Tagore is one of continuity and contrast; but as mentioned at the beginning of the first chapter, it is far from comprehensive, and much room lies vacant for many more translations. Another mode of translation historiography is also to examine different statements about translation made in different languages as well as English. Similarly "The Two-Worlds Theory", which articulates shifting terms in the relationship between 'Indian languages' and English could also take account of relationships (if any) between inter-regional and English translation. This involves the ideological implications and repercussions of English translation activity on intra-regional translation activity. Since this subject requires careful examination, we shall revert to it later.

The chapter 'Within Academia' points to fresh areas of inquiry, especially for teachers and academics. Although translation scholars like Vanamala Viswanath have demonstrated usefulness of translation as a pedagogical tool, much work still needs to be done. How are translation courses to be framed and taught in a multilingual classroom? Should IWE and ILET be part of the same course, inadequately titled 'Literature in English?' If, as Venuti argues, "Reading a translation as a translation means reflecting on its conclusions, the domestic dialects and discourses in which it is written and the domestic cultural situation in which it is read" (1995:312). Then how does a Bengali-speaking teacher teach a text translated from Malayalam? Do translations of Indian literatures in English require more indigenous translation theory and would a more 'liberal' and 'Indian' (if you will) translation also enlarge Indian literature in English by including adaptations and transcreations?

In the chapter 'Outside the Discipline' interconnections between translation activity and parallel developments in related print and visual media could not include the productive exchange between translated texts and the televised role of subtitling and dubbing as acts of translation. Technological advances in 'regional' computer software or the availability and increase of 'regional' channels may work as counter-processes to the use of English language. Once again, it is important to comment, but too early to conclude here. In the meanwhile there are a few more English-language publishers involved now (especially since 2002) in English translation activity and it has not been possible to include them. Students interested in literary translation or even the relationship between sociology and publishing could examine the role of editors who provide vision and make a difference in the publishing scene.

It remains to take account of certain problematic issues that pursue English translation activity in India. The most important of these has to do with the ideological implications of English translations. The social importance of English helps enhance the regional text and its author. Thus translation is crucial not only because it makes, say, Gujarati writers available to non-Gujarati readers, but also because it enhances the importance of the Gujarati writers themselves. Noted Tamil writer C.S. Lakshmi says, "I have been writing for many years in Tamil, but it is only after I have been translated into English that I am invited to forums like this. So, being translated into English was actually a kind of promotion. Because, when you write only in Tamil, they assume that you don't have anything to state"(in *The Book Review I*, 1997). This itself is a strong comment on the Indian middle class intelligentsia, for whom "only the literary document produced in English is a national document; all else is regional, hence minor and forgettable, so that English emerges in this imagination, not as one of the Indian languages, which it undoubtedly is, but as the language of national integration and bourgeois civility" (Ahmad, 1994:75).

There are a number of crucial questions yet to be grappled with, such as: Do translations in English affect or obliterate interregional activity? Does translation into English perpetuate the dominance of English over the bhashas? What kind of representation of 'Indian reality' is made through English translation?

These questions may be considered under the rubric of asymmetrical power relations. We first turn to the question of interregional translation, that is, the effect of English translation upon translations from one bhasha into another. Both the Sahitya Akademi and more especially the National Book Trust through its scheme benignly called *Aadan-Pradan* ('Give and take') are concerned with translations from one Indian language into another. Despite the government backing provided to these two institutions, not much seems to have been done in the field of inter-regional translation. Indra Nath Chaudhury remarks that "Through an assessment made of translations done in India from 1875 to 1990, it has been discovered that only a few translations are made from one Indian language to another of good literature" (1998). Chaudhury maintains that there are three reasons behind this. First, there is general apathy among writers insofar as accepting translation as a major literary activity, and second, there are not many people who know languages other than their own and third, there is the problem of marketing 'regional language' books per se, let alone translated books. One may conclude from Chaudhury's observations that the paucity of translations from one language into another is not an outcome of translations into English. However, it is ungainsayable that the networks of distribution and prominence available to English-language activity are not available to regional language publishing.

"Translation into English is part of a worldwide circuit of cultural exchange" (Bellos 1997:339). The impact of ILET and the representational claims it makes are to be viewed not in the context of an Indian market alone, but also in the context of the world-market. Translation wields enormous power in constructing representations of foreign culture. It has very often changed, for better or worse, the perception of the source culture, and helped sustain stereotypes (as in the case of *Gitanjali*) or even, in some cases, erode them. Various kinds of texts have been translated: social realism (e.g. *Paraja* and *Samskara*) with a strong emphasis upon the caste-system; women's texts (the works of Ismat Chugtai and Mahasweta Devi); radical verse of the *vacana* kind (*Says Tuka* and the *Songs of Mira*). Is the story of 'orientalist' translations being repeated in a neo-colonial world? Trivedi warns against such positioning when he says:

> The ultimate question before us in India ...is where to situate ourselves
> and our literary culture vis-à-vis the new post-colonial global cultural con-
> figuration. Are we going to align ourselves, sooner rather than later, with
> the great Anglo-American axis, as a nation and a people who read and
> write only in English? Or do we have the strength of our local earthy smells
> to hold out against this linguistic and cultural totalization, this increasing
> monolingual literary authoritarianism? In this case shall we wait to be trans-
> lated into English or any other language on our own terms, as do China,
> Japan, East Europe and Latin America? (1996:54)

It is necessary to attend to Trivedi's note of caution and the cultural implications
of English translation although Trivedi overstates the case. It is essential to admit that the dynamic nature of this industry has grown not simply to slake the
West's thirst for an exotic India, but also as a profound response to the sociological truth of our own lives. Having said that, it may be useful to see English
through translation as a space or a forum made inescapable through dominance
as well democracy. In other words, English through translation provides a plat-
form which different utterances of linguistic and cultural and political persuasions
simultaneously inhabit. English neither 'binds' them (a la traditional view of
translation as a humanistic tool) nor divides them (as detractors of English maintain). It serves as an alternative space that on one hand consolidates the hegemony
of English, while on the other makes it also relatively free of upper-caste and
low-caste, language and dialect oppositions. Theoretically and potentially speaking, English translation can embrace the metropolitan as well as the rural
(however inadequately), un/recognized languages, written and oral, upper-caste
and dalit/tribal/subaltern works and yet meet the needs of a wide market. No
other 'pan-Indian' language is this acceptable to different sections whose cause
English is expected to 'represent'. Unlike Sanskrit which carries the memory of
caste domination, English can also represent, argues S. Anand, a "dalit bahujan
[subaltern groups] standpoint" and "help us imagine Indian unity" (see Dasgupta
2000, 1407). English is a space "where foundations for sustainable solidarities
can be built... especially by dalit bahujans pooling together nationally their regional trajectories and strategies". This is one of the many instances by which
English by itself and also through translation finds justification. It also seeks to
highlight fresh equations that English is likely to make with 'Indian languages'
especially through translation.

Finally, *Translating India* takes its cue from Indian scholars involved in
para-literary forces of translation theory, especially Sujit Mukherjee and G.N.
Devy. It also aligns itself with the historical approach employed by Jean Delisle
and Judith Woodsworth (1995) on one hand and the polysystem view of translation expounded by Itamar Zohar and Gideon Toury (The discussion of publishing
strategies and various ideologies of translation gain from Theo Hermans (1985),
Raniner Schulte (1990) and Lawrence Venuti (1992, 1995, 2000). At the same
time, *Translating India* departs from previous works by its overemphasis upon
sociological contexts. And yet much soil lies uncovered within this fertile ground.

Appendix 1

This section contains the questionnaire that was handed out or mailed to select publishers before the actual interview. During the interview, some questions were modified according to the publishing priorities of each publisher and some new questions emerged on the basis of my dialogue with publishers.

1. What has been the effect of liberalization post 1991 in the publishing industry?
2. Who are the major players in the Indian publishing industry?
3. What is the pattern of distribution in India? What are the margins at various levels?
4. Do you import books published by your principals and distribute them in India? Similarly, does your principal distribute books published by you in India?
5. What are the patterns of consumption? Where is your market located – small towns/metropolises; individuals/institutions?
6. There has been a significant rise in English-language publishing in the last decade or so. Are there any specific government policies you attribute this to?
7. Which other factors seem responsible to you for this increase in English-language books?
8. In recent times English-language books have received a lot of coverage in book promoting journals. Has this affecting your sales in any significant way?
9. Approximately how many books do you publish annually?
10. What percentage of your output consists of texts in translation?
11. When did you first publish a translated work in India? Title.
12. Which languages have you published these texts from and what are your criteria for selection?
13. What are your mechanisms for testing quality translations?
14. Is publishing Indian literature in English translation an economically viable business for you?
15. What are the rates of payment as far as translators are concerned? Do they have copyrights?
16. How does the hierarchy in the tripartite scheme of publisher-writer-translator operate?
17. What percentage or units of books are exported abroad and to whom? Is there a market abroad for translated texts?

Appendix 2

Appendix 2 provides full transcripts of my interviews with publishers. The interviews are preceded by some factual details about each publishing house. The gist of these interviews is interwoven into one of the sections in 'Publishers' Perspective'.

Transcripts have not been provided, however, for informal interviews conducted with:
G. N. Devy, 15 Sept. 1997
Bholabhai Patel, 1 Oct. 1997
Ramlal Parikh, 1 Oct. 1997
Yashwant Shukla, 1 Oct. 1997
Harish Trivedi, 15 Feb. 1998
Gaurav Shah, 15 Jan 1999

Sahitya Akademi

The Akademi was set up in 1954 by the Government of India to meet the challenges of a multilingual society and foster art and literature of the Indian people. The Akademi has been trying to meet this challenge in two ways: firstly by producing informative material regarding literary activities in all Indian languages and secondly by publishing translations of award-winning titles from one Indian language into another. The Akademi started off as national organization that would, among many other things, subsidize the cost of books which normally do not interest private publishers. This noble, but perhaps unrealistic, aim had to be amended in course of time because the private publishers never showed any interest in Sahitya Akademi projects. In course of time, the Akademi had to start publishing and marketing its own books. At the same time, the pricing structure in Sahitya Akademi is different from that of private publishers. The Akademi does not take into account the cost of preparation of a manuscript, i.e. the remuneration paid to the author/compiler/translator/reviser, because such expenditure is a part of the literary activities of the Sahitya Akademi, is treated as subsidy in the larger national interest. As a result, the Akademi's investment in promoting and advertising books is also low and this very often results in poor sales of its books.

   Given below is an interview with the Secretary of the Sahitya Akademi, Prof. K. Satchidanandan taken on 27 December 1997.

1. Private publishers these days have been taking a lot of interest in translations. In the light of this, do you think the role and usefulness of the Akademi is called into question?
No I don't think so. The Sahitya Akademi is still a very valuable organization.

The private publishers are interested only in marketable books. Their concerns are essentially concerns of the market. In that sense, there might be avant-garde books that they will not publish. But we can afford to take those risks. New trends need a lot of encouragement.

2. Are you saying that the Sahitya Akademi is freer than private publishers when it come to selecting books?

Our organization is free from the logic of the market – it has more space for maneuvering.

3. Theoretically speaking, the Akademi has a uniform language policy and is committed to ensuring an equal representation of all languages. Does that happen in practice? Do you think some languages are more privileged than some others?

The distribution of representation is almost equal. I say almost equal because the wealth of literature and language has to be taken into account. Some languages appear richer (such as Bengali or Marathi) in terms of a more advanced sensibility. The literary histories in some languages are products of long courses of evolution. These differences are reflected in the number of books coming from a language. And yet we do translations from all recognized languages into Hindi and English first and then subsequently into other languages. Our work goes beyond the 22 languages – into what are called dialects.

4. What makes some languages more visible than others? How are perceptions about a language being rich or not rich formed?

It could be, as I said, because of older literary traditions, levels of literacy and economics etc. At times we also find certain languages more assertive and successful in capturing attention. There has been a concerted effort to promote Bengali. Even mediocre works from Bengali get more attention than say Sindhi or Gujarati.

5. Do the state akademis also publish translations in English or is it the purview only of the Central Akademi? If there are more works being translated from a language, is it that the State Akademi there has played an active role?

State Akademis have published books in English but because of the lack of distribution they remain unnoticed. They find it difficult to compete with efficient systems of private publishers. But you are right, some State Akademis are quite active. The Malyalam (which I have known closely) State Akademi has published quite a few translations.

6. What are your translation programs? Do you translate book that has received an award?

We have a scheme for the translation of such books. There has been an amendment in the policy of translating all award-winning books. All these books are not very great books. We are obliged to give one award every year to every language. But it is not necessary to translate that book into all the 22 languages. We have decided to make a select list of award-winning books, leave the decision to the advisory board. Every five years we form an advisory board. Only they know what will be received outside their language. We are also thinking of forming a national committee that will recommend the best books from all parts of the country. Their recommendations may include award-winning books too.

7. What is your mode of distribution?
We sell our books through individual orders, bulk buyers, railways, and the external affairs department. The Sahitya Akademi has agencies in England, U.S. and Canada. We also participate in all major book- exhibitions. We organize annual exhibitions at the Sahitya Akademi. Most of our books get sold, depending upon the language we sell.

8. In the last five to ten years have any new developments with respect to translation occurred?
Some changes have occurred in the Akademi's translation programs after the eighties. Our workshops for literary translation have become more systematic. In 1996 we established a translation center called Shabdana. This centre organizes seminars and workshops on the theory of translation and invites translators known the world over. The aim is to arrive at some kind of Indian theory of translation. We are also trying to fill some gaps in literary history by now focussing on Prachya series – literature post-medieval and pre-modern. We have also instituted now a prize for translation.

9. Does most of your work take place through English or through Hindi?
We use both. But we find English more acceptable in South India.

Macmillan

Macmillan (India) was always a subsidiary concern of Macmillan U.K. Macmillan in India began to represent Macmillan of Britain in 1902. Hence the Indian concern has not had a completely Indian ownership. For a very brief spell after 1979, when foreign holdings had to be reversed in favour of Indian ownership, the parent company's equity holding was 40 percent. Again in 1994, Macmillan U.K. acquired majority holding in the company. In the case of Macmillan, ownership of the company by the foreign partner has not determined the rules, policies, and publishing programs of the Indian subsidiary. Macmillan (India) runs as an Indian company in its outlook, content, and policies. Macmillan (India) focuses primarily on educational and academic books.

Given below is an interview with Mini Krishnan, the general editor at

Macmillan who has been the main force behind the Macmillan's recent series of Modern Indian Novels in Translation.The interview was conducted on 13 April 1998.

1. What has been the publishing thrust of Macmillan India so far?
Macmillan (in India) is primarily an academic publisher, specializing in textbooks actually. That's where our bread and butter lie.

2. What has been the effect of liberalization post 1991 on the publishing
     industry?
A lot of foreign publishers have come seeking the world's largest English knowing and reading (if not actually buying) audience. They have found that it's a very price sensitive market and they can hope to only make up in volume what they cannot achieve through high prices. This has often meant using local printers so that business has boomed. Apart from this business/commerce growth has resulted in more glamorous image-building and that in turn has led to any number of DTP (Desk Top Publishing) operators, graphic, designers, people who may be said to be on the publishing periphery. Also many people are going into various niche markets.

3. Who are the major players in the market today?
Surely Oxford University Press India, Macmillan India, Tata-Mcgraw, Orient Longman, and Prentice-Hall. There are publishers who get into the limelight a lot but who are not actually making that much money. Penguin India, HarperCollins, Rupa... it's with a backbone of academic and educational publishing that publishers make big money.

4. There has been a significant rise in English-language publishing in the
     last decade or so. Are there any specific government policies you at-
     tribute this to?
Actually government policy has been weighted against English language publishing. State textbook societies have been doing their best to take this away from private publishers but since this is an area where they (government bodies) are not willing to invest time and expertise, it really is the only subject that private publishers are still able to hang on to. But because India is so science and technology driven and for that you need a sort of English as you do for computer sciences, you have the continuing importance of English.

5. Which other factors seem responsible to you for this increase in English-
     language books?
There is a larger and larger population of language orphans. People migrating away from their home states may not have the time or energy to make certain that their children know their mother tongue as well as they knows English. So you have a growing body of youngsters who know one or two Indian languages to speak but only English to read and write in.

6. What kind of circumstances and observations about the market made
    Macmillan undertake this project of translation?

I set about planning these translations in 1984-85. Before the 90s we had some
idealistic leaders who signed up books like Comparative Indian literature. When
I had to publish that I thought to myself here is critical matter on every genre of
16 languages but where are the primary texts? And will they EVER be studied
unless we bring them into translation? And if we've been studying Tagore for
decades in English Literature courses in translation why not some of our other
writers?

7. Has publishing translation been economically viable for you?

The most important item of survival is money. I don't believe that translations
are lucrative unless you get one or two titles into university board prescriptions
every year. Translations rarely pay for themselves. Hence our translations are
targeted towards home audiences, students and foreign readers. My concern
was how best to make it possible for these translations to be both enjoyable
reading material and textbook design?

8. A.R. Educational Trust has sponsored the Macmillan series? What made
    you seek an outside body for funding?

Macmillan did not want to give up its textbook program at the cost of these
translations. They had reservations about putting money into a project where
financial returns are not easy to come by. So I had to go for funding outside. In
effect I have been doing two jobs – the translations and the textbooks.

9. Have these translations been prescribed in any academic courses?

They have been prescribed in Women's Christian College, Madras; Bharathi
Dasan University, Coimbatore, Madras University's MA – the open credit course.
Four novels from Macmillan's! *The Eye of God*, *Subarnalata*, then *Face of the
Morning* and *Yamini*. and the other prescriptions in various universities men-
tioned above are again *The Eye of God*, *Yamini* and *Lamps in the Whirlpool*.

10. Has there been an overseas market for this series of Indian Novels in
    Translation?

Macmillan U.K have broken all existing historical records and lifted 200 copies
of all the 18 titles we have done so far and distributed them through UK and
Europe. I think the time is not far when translations will sell massively because
India is very trendy and a lot of people seriously want to understand our country.

11. In recent times English-language books have received a lot of coverage in
    book promoting journals. Has this affected your sales in any significant
    way?

Yes indeed there is always a spurt in sales following any kind of publicity. We
get letters and calls even months later when someone sees the magazine in a
dentist's waiting room or something!

12. What have been your philosophy and goal as far as translation is
     concerned?

Our philosophy has been to show as authentic a picture as possible of the different strata of Indian society. No packaging. Make available explanations for Indian
words that won't translate. Don't pretend they don't exist. If someone wants to
understand our country and culture (which we ourselves find difficult to understand) he/she must get a glimpse of it from our fiction – just as the social history
of England is seen in Galsworthy and Iris Murdoch.

13. What are your mechanisms for testing the quality of translations?

I work very very closely with the author and translator and, if the chief editor is
willing, with him/her too. I also show drafts to potential readers. I make a great
effort to edit the material, asking for footnotes, and trying to get good academic
introductions written. Readability seems to be a bad word. It should not be.

Katha

Initiated by Geeta Dharmarajan in 1988 as a not-for-profit organization, it is the
first of its kind in India. It is a decentralized organization with interdependent
cells for research and publication that want to meet the challenges of a multi-
linguistic nation. The objectives of Katha are at two levels, literacy and literature.
Kalpavriksham is Katha's Center for Sustainable Learning and it engages in
evolving new, innovative reading apparatus for children and adults. Katha is
also engaged in other kinds of developmental work in the areas of social and
gender inequalities. Kathavilasam functions at the level of literature. Through
Kathavilasam Katha aims at "applauding good literature", especially short stories, by making it available through translation.

Interview with Geeta Dharmarajan on 11 April, 1998.

1. What is the philosophy underlying the organization Katha?

Katha is a registered non-profit organization. Our main objective is to enhance
the pleasures of reading, to showcase literary creativity. Our philosophy is that
at the beginning of everything is the story. That lifelong learning for all of us
began with the story heard sitting on a favourite grandmother's lap, the heaving
stomach of a grandfather. We believe the story promotes creativity in all fields,
from science to art.

It enhances the quality of life, gives us a lasting sense of ethics, and values
for life, for all life forms, for diverse cultures, peoples. In this age of the global
village, a true understanding of a people can not come from understanding their
technology. It can only come from a deep understanding of the way their minds
work, through characters, through stories.

2. How would you compare the role and aims of Katha with, say, the Sahitya Akademi?

(Apart from the fact that the Sahitya Akademi is a state-funded body etc.)

i.   Katha sees the need to promote reading as the single most important act in India today. The basic difference between Katha and other publishers, state or otherwise, may be that we are interested in reading, in readers, in making reading a sustainable activity. We want people to read books. Since writers write books, writers become important. For example, the Katha Award is for Creative Fiction; it is not given to the writer, but to a story. Bodies like the Sahitya Akademi are into promoting writers, primarily.

ii. We see this our books as being primarily for the Indian reader who wants to read what is being written today in the various languages that she/he cannot read.

iii. Katha's spectrum is broader than any other organization we know of. We work in the literacy to literature continuum. We see literature as fun and as a relevant tool in working in women's empowerment, in children's education, or in holistic and sustainable development – all areas in which Katha is presently working.

iv. Being a small, voluntary organization, we work through the Friends of Katha network. The KathaNet has some 4000 friends who seem ready to spontaneously do anything to promote their languages, their literatures. We have been focussing on short fiction till now.

v.   We do not have the kind of funds that a state organization like the Sahitya Akademi has; but unnecessary baggage like regional representation, etc. does not hamstring us either.

vi. We could not see italics as the magic device one sometimes wishes for that can give meaning to words. So, in Katha, we use italics only for emphasis, not to differentiate a word from a bhasha that has been retained from the source language.

vii. Every story we have published (except in the YuvaKatha series) has been translated specially for Katha. Perhaps Katha in India started the new trend of not 'borrowing' from other publications?

3. Katha's has been a success story. Had Katha been set up twenty or thirty years ago, do you think it would have still been successful? What role has the post-80s context played in this?

As Victor Hugo (?) said, "You can resist an invading army, but not an idea whose time has come". I believe the time has come for Indian literature in quality translation!

    The post-80s scenario in colleges and schools has seen the dismaying movement away from a true liberal education, of the kind that Dr Radhakrishnan talked of and wanted for us, as also the growing influence of television. Western values and entertainment are larger than life for most of us. Hence Indian literature which is home-bred seems irrelevant, not fun. I must say I feel a little dismayed by our own lack of knowledge of our own writers and their writings. In one college I visited, students had problems understanding the culture of a language and people who had been their close neighbours for the last 2000 years, if not more! Yet, these same students had no problems understanding Marquez, Calvino or the American writers. We have been able to appreciate the 'magic realism' of the Latin American writers, but have no time for the fantasy of the Indian epics.

But I think the need for Indian literature is stronger. Unless we are deeply and firmly rooted in our own culture and beliefs and values, we cannot perform and stand up to be counted in the real world outside. Hence, the greater need today for our own literatures, and the magic of words that our Indian writers weave with the everydayness of rural, urban Indian life.

This is the reason Katha has been working with school and college students, through workshops and good quality publications, we hope to recreate the interest in our languages, in translations, that was there in the ancient universities of Nalanda and Kanchi.

4.   Why has Katha been interested only in short fiction?
I have believed that the genius of India's literary talent lies in its short fiction rather than in the novel. If poetry had been in vogue, I would have said poetry/ epics. Hence Katha's interest in the short story.

Also, having been in the field for the last ten years, I do think that the shorter form is easier to read, captures a brilliance that is of a different order than in the novel, and dazzles often with its brevity, its encapsulated characterization.

5.   What role have awards played in boosting up the image, sales, and quality of translation in Katha?
The Awards have made a difference for especially the younger, emerging writers. Katha was the first body to recognize the role of translators and that they were as important as writers, in a country like India.

Katha gave the first awards for translators, much earlier than even the Sahitya Akademi did. And the Katha Journal Award is, even today, the only one of its kind. It recognizes editors who give space to quality short fiction. So also the Katha AK Ramanujan Award that is given to a translator who, with felicity and grace, can translate from more than one Indian languages.

I think the image of Katha has been built up not so much because of the awards, but because of the quality of our stories/writing in the source language, our in-house editing, and production. We have been coming out consistently with winners I think (thanks to our Nominating Editors) and this has built up the status of the Awards in the eyes of the reading public. Also, when we started, the quality of translations we got was not up to the mark. This has improved vastly today. And this is definitely due to the Awards.

6. When stories are selected/nominated/translated, what criteria are they
    based upon?

We have always had a Nominating Editor for each language, someone who not
only knows his or her language and literature well, but who will actively support our cause, as a labour of love. For the Katha Awards, they are asked to
select three stories each from those that have been published by a quality conscious editor in the preceding year. The conscious decision to have an eclectic
process so that the diverse tastes of editors of diverse magazines and journals
(ranging from a popular commercial weekly that sells in the lakhs, to a quiet
small magazine with a dedicated band of readers) have only added to the richness of the collection.

We do not even try to represent all the Indian languages. The writers and
scholars who accepted to be our nominating editors have determined this. I would
like to stress here that we try to steer clear of the politics of language and translation. The fact that we are going into a 'language of power' makes writers
accept even bad translations easily sometimes. We find the need to be scrupu-
lously honest in our dealings with language to avoid any embarrassments for the
writers. We also strive to include as many women writers as possible, without
compromising on quality or excellence, of course.

As for translations, I had said in our first volume that there is a need for
more translators. It was for this specific reason, to enlarge the pool of quality
translators, that Katha devised and carried out the First All-India Translation
Contest where we had more than 1200 people participating. Done with a grant
from the British Council, the donors got such good feedback that they asked us
if we could do the Second All-India Translation Contest. We did this, with an
overwhelming response again, (1700 entries). Now, for a third round, we have
suggested a SAARC Translation Contest. This is onstream now!

Have Katha publications been prescribed in academic courses at colleges
and universities?

They are being used in Madras University, we are told. IGNOU has used
some we hear. Other major publishers of academic books have picked up our
stories for inclusion in selections.

7. Which target groups does Katha address?

We try giving good quality Indian literature to the common reader who is already in the habit of reading. We have focussed a lot on class-room learning and
teaching of literature in translation. Hence the attempt to go into schools and
colleges. The Kanchi Initiative at Katha focuses attention on students and teachers
of language. Through the last year, we have had workshops in Teaching Translation for TEACHERS in Delhi University, Jaipur University, Amritsar, Madras,
Madurai and Tirunelveli. We have also started a Teachers' Resource Centre that
will have primary, secondary and supporting materials on Indian writers to fa-
cilitate the teaching of their writings in language classrooms. Katha has launched

Dhammak Dhum! This is India's first magazine for primary school children, which places emphasis on Indian poems and stories in translation.

8. What do you have to say about Katha's decision to use English as a unifying language? What are the ideological implications of this?

We do not see English as a 'unifying language'. We started publishing in English so as to be able to be in publishing. Having no godfather/corpus/government backing, we have had to stand on our own from the start. But we have always striven to get our stories translated into as many languages as possible. We also publish in many languages: Bangla, Kannada, Tamil, and Urdu. We publish for neo-literates in up to six Indian languages: Hindi, Gujarati, Kannada, Malayalam, Telugu, and Urdu.

But we do see English as one of the Indian languages. We have published from over 13 Indian languages into English, as can be seen from the fact that we have always had the Katha Award for creative Writing in English.

9. What has been your experience of working with various languages? Do you think some languages are more amenable to translation than some others (in terms of availability of bilinguals, high levels of literacy/education etc).

While working on our various collections, we have asked ourselves many questions. Are many languages living on their past glories? Are short story writers being lured into quick money and fame by writing the serialized novel for pulp magazines? Are they being overwhelmed by 'true' stories appearing in regional newspapers which through clever use of language, fantasize the real with support from 'relevant' photography? Have publishers shied away from publishing short fiction because there aren't enough good stories?

I believe that all Indian bhashas have an affinity and a shared culture base that makes translation between them easier than translation into English. But there are (amazingly!) more people who can go between one bhasha and English than between two bhashas!

In terms of tools also, we find there are more dictionaries etc between the bhashas and English, than between two bhashas. Of the languages, in our limited knowledge, we find that Gujarati and Telugu seem to have fewer persons translating into English. So also with Konkani and Oriya.

Penguin India

Penguin India started in India in 1985. Penguin is responsible for introducing organized and cohesive publishing programmes in literary and commercial fiction. It also publishes other genres such as biographies, autobiographies, and travelogues. Translations still form 15 per cent of the output with Penguin India.

The interview below with Zamir Ansari, Marketing Manager, Penguin

India Ltd. on 29 December 1997 will bear a few facts out:

1. What has been the effect of liberalization post-1991 on the publishing
    industry?

Liberalization means nothing to the publishers. It means perhaps we will now
be able to import newsprint, paper, and machinery. It may improve the material
conditions of publishing. But apart from that it does not mean much.

2. What have been the publishing thrust and philosophy of Penguin India?

Penguin India's main thrust has been in Indian writing in English. Before Penguin India entered the Indian scene in 1985, there were Indian authors published
here by Rupa or Jaico and imported Pocket books also had something to do with
Indian writing in English. But all that was done sporadically. There was no
visible body. After Penguin India authors like Vikram Seth have chosen to be
first published here. In these ten years there is a sea-change as far as Indian
Writing in English is concerned.

3. What about translations? How do they fare? Do they make an economi-
    cally viable activity?

Translations are of two kinds, classical and contemporary. We translate from
classical languages such as Sanskrit and Persian. We also translate from contemporary Indian works. Penguin U.K has had a long distinguished career in
classical translations. Even now our classical language translations do very well,
at least in the international market. They get prescribed for Comparative Literature courses in the U.S. It is easier to find classics. Because there are scholars
who have been published. There is access to body of literature that is available.
Also we had the advantage of being a part of Penguin U.K. Classics in translation was a very distinguished activity with Penguin U.K. We knew where the
wealth lay. Unfortunately translations do not travel. Contemporary translations
have not met with great success. Quite a few people would have either read the
original or end up comparing it with the original. Unless there is something of
universal appeal like Satyajit Ray's Feluda Stories. But you take the case of
Gujarati, *Seven Steps to the Sky*. It has done well, but good reviews and selling
2000 copies do not success make. How do you rate success? Unless the book
continues to remain on the shelf and goes into reprint, unless there is continuity
and the success translates into sales. In many cases translations leave a lot to be
desired.

4. What is Penguin India's relationship with the principal company? Does
    your principal firm import books from here?

Penguin India represents Penguin U.K. It's a joint venture – they are the majority share holders. They import books from here, but they choose titles.

5. In recent times English-language books have received a lot of coverage

in book promoting journals. Has this been affecting your sales in any significant way?

All leading newspapers and journals now carry reviews and advertisements on books. Except for *Times of India* which has discontinued its literary page, almost all dailies including *The Hindustan Times, The Telegraph, The Hindu, The Express* carry extracts and reviews. Journals like *The Indian Review of Books* have sales figures of 5000 copies. Then there are *India Today* and *Outlook* and now finally door to door mail. All this has made our task easier and the customer's task easier.

6.   Which source languages have you chosen for your translations?

We have translated from Hindi, Urdu, Malyalam, Tamil, Telugu and I think, Sanskrit. We have not translated from Oriya. We can do wherever there is editorial expertise available. In our own office we have Hindi, Bengali, Malyalam, Urdu.

7.   What are your means for testing the quality of translations?

We get them reviewed by our editorial staff, which is why we have to restrict ourselves to a few languages. We could get outside reviewers to assess translations, but then the cost becomes high.

8.   What have been your successful translations, in terms of constant demand?

Our successful translations have been those of Sadat Hussain Manto, Satyajit Ray, and Bankimchandra. Translations from Urdu sell very well, anything related to the experience of Partition. Also Faiz is very much in vogue. If we had to mention one book in translation that has kind of changed the course for us, then it is Satyajit Ray's Feluda Stories. I suppose it has a universal appeal.

9.   Do you export to other countries?

We do some. It's just that there are so many bureaucratic problems in India about everything. On the whole we always end up doing less than we can. Talking of exports – we could export much more to our neighbouring countries – Pakistan, for instance. But the bilateral agreement between India and Pakistan allows only scientific/technical/educational/religious books. As a market we are self-restrictive.

10. How much do you pay your translators?

Translators anywhere in the world about 5 per cent of the cover price, if the payment is on a royalty basis. If it's a lump-sum payment then it all depends – five thousand to ten thousand. Royalty can be as low as 2 per cent and never exceeds 7 per cent. Margins at every level are very low. Publishing is a precarious business. You have to make a choice. Either you print 1000 copies at 250 or 300 each and break even or you publish 2000 copies.

Oxford University Press

OUP as it is better known, like Macmillan, is primarily an educational publisher. It has been an educational and academic publisher with the 100 per cent ownership of the Oxford University Press, U.K. Its focus was almost exclusively on educational and academic books till 1970. The general list in OUP began after the 70s. OUP (U.K.) imports all the published titles in varying quantities depending upon the demand there. Presented below is an interview held Rukun Advani, the chief editor at OUP, on 29 December, 1997.

1. What have been your philosophy and involvement as far translations from regional languages into English are concerned?

We have not actively chased or commissioned translations. If someone approaches us, someone we know, then we publish translations. By and large there is large number of books that can be translated, but we are not in a position to choose and undertake major translation programs. Given our editorial priorities, we cannot actively engage in translations.

2. Approximately how many books do you publish annually? What percentage of your output consists of texts in translation?

Very small. It's a hit or miss thing. Our annual output is of 175 new titles, 35 paperbacks of which about 2-3 are translations. It's a very meagre output and subject to the availability of good translations.

3. Why such meagre output?

We are very finicky, very fussy. Unless something is exceptionally good as an English rendering we do not like to publish. There is a fair amount of translation available, if one is willing to be more flexible. We could have more translations on our list if we were to believe that it is important for translations to come out initially. And that is a legitimate feeling. But we tend to play very safe.

4. What are your mechanisms for testing quality?

We have an in-house reviewer and one outside reviewer. We show our translations to people who know the Source Language and are impeccably fluent in English. For instance, when Gopinath Mohanty's *Paraja* translated by Bikram Das came to us – it was an unknown, unfamiliar text. We showed it to Amitav Ghosh and his recommendation was instrumental in publishing it – after a lot of vetting, drafting, and revising. Similarly, we published Ramanujan because we knew him and *Samskara* was a well-known book.

5. The first work in translation you published was Tagore's Three Plays (1950), the next work appears only in 1972, Karnad's Tughlaq. Why was there such a long gap between the two?

As I said earlier, OUP in the 1950s was an educational publisher. We did not
have a general list at all. Tagore's *Three Plays* was a college text and that is how
it must have been published. Subsequently our general publishing began in the
early seventies when RaviDayal came. That was when we published Girish
Karnad. Girish Karnad worked with the OUP, so that helped. Then the poets
Parthasarthy and Ramanujan joined. That's how we got *Samskara* and the plays.
We recently published Tendulkar's *Five Plays* in a collection and also *Kanyadaan*.
We have signed a contract for Girish Karnad's latest play, *Fire and Rain* and
Premchand 's *Nirmala* translated by Alok Rai.

6. In purely publishing terms, what has it meant publishing translations by
    Ramanujan? Has his standing as the most known translator affected the
    sales figures of his books?

The sales figures of Ramanujan's translations are very good. Every time we
publish anything by Ramanujan – it is a guarantee. Not just immediate sales, but
it remains a lot on the list for a long time. Ultimately these things filter into
courses. Particularly now with a shift from mainstream British literature to indigenous literatures. Ramanujan's own output changed the translation map
because as far as ancient texts were concerned they were only Sanskrit texts.

7. OUP first took the lead in bringing out Modern Drama in India. Why did
    it never go beyond the four major language-communities – Tendulkar
    (Marathi), Karnad (Kannada). Badal Sircar (Bengali). What happened to
    that project?

It is only because our publishing has focussed very largely on academic/ scholarly literature in economics and sociology. Given our editorial focus we have
and are obliged to focus on these areas. Also we did not have a literary editor for
a long time. Also because we are very finicky. So people tend to migrate in other
directions.

8. Is publishing translations economically viable? Is there a market now for
    translations?

There is a steady local market for translations. It is not a huge market, in our
perspective. The huge market is still with anthologies that keep getting prescribed for courses. For example, Arvind Krishna Mehrotra's anthology of Indian
English poets gets sold in thousands – 30,000 to 60,000 copies. So we are not
talking of those numbers as far as translations are concerned. Translations are
usually MA texts here in Delhi or Calcutta, or sometimes some select American
universities. We sell maximum 2000 copies. So in commercial terms it is a very
small number and it does not make a very fruitful business – which is why not
many people want to invest in this kind of activity.

9. What kinds of constraints do you face by being a university press (com-
    pared to a fully commercial publisher like Penguin)?

There are constraints to being a university publisher. The constraints are what I said earlier, quality consciousness, extremely cautious publishing plans, and low pricing. We cannot price our books very high which means each unit costs a lot and the recovery is that much less.

10. Is there an overseas market for translations?
Translations do fairly well overseas – not exceptionally well. More so in the U.S. Less in the U.K. The U.S. has a large contingent of Indian academics. For example, Menon's translation of Urdu short stories have done reasonably well because it has been prescribed in some course. Again Menon teaches in Wisconsin. That must have helped. I mentioned Gopinath Mohanty's *Paraja*. We sell 700-800 copies of *Paraja* every year to Cornell University. Gopinath Mohanty's son Satya Mohanty teaches there. *Samskara* has done very well because it is a part of courses on Hinduism. Also Ramanujan was in Chicago. It's quite a help if someone in an institution supports you. Many Indian academics teaching History in American Universities use fiction as an entry point to Indian History. Such shifts have parallels in many ways.

11. Are you saying then that there is a lot of interdependence between academic institutions and publishing houses, especially in an activity like this?
You see in India, by and large people buy a book if it is prescribed or if it has a utility. We sell something like Mehrotra's *Twelve Modern Indian Poets* – 1500 copies a year because it is prescribed. It is very important for these texts to be part of some kind of canon, some kind of re-thinking which is going on in the universities or is required for passing exams, then there is a market. Shifts in academic institutions are very necessary, publishers then follow suit. We can only make things available and hope that they will get prescribed. We can be instrumental in a limited way, make it available and hope that it will be incorporated into the syllabus. Here and there we strike lucky. Initially we are just making an investment in the hope of some future gain.

12. Is there a future in the publication of translations?
The future seem reasonably good, especially because there is repositioning and questioning of the canon in the universities. There is a shift onto central ground of what was earlier on the margins. Once these shifts are accelerated, there will be a larger market for translations.

Rupa-HarperCollins

Rupa is a very old company which for years was engaged in direct publishing as well as reprinting imported books. The tie-up between Rupa and HarperCollins took place in 1991. The Indian partner is dominant in the 60/40 arrangement. Co-publishing has resulted in books of a very mixed nature. Rupa-HarperCollins perceives the marketability of authors as being more important not so much the fact that they are Indians or Western. The general list includes almost all genres of trade publishing – travelogues, biographies, children's books, Indian writing in English and of course translations.

An interview taken on 30 December 1997 with the editor Renuka Chatterjee follows:

1.   What has been the effect of liberalization on the English publishing industry?

It has not had a drastic effect. There is a perception that because the economy has opened up, overseas publishers will start operations here. Those rumours have been around for five years now. But I don't see that happening because the market for English readers still has to grow. The market for English books is far too small to interest a foreign publisher. It's only about 2 million. Indian publishers like Penguin and us find it difficult to go beyond a print-run of 2000-3000. If we sell anything between 5000-10,000 we consider it a bestseller. So until the readership grows, I don't think there are any chances of multinationals coming in.

2.   There is a lot of prominence as far as English books by Indian authors are concerned? What do you attribute this to?

There is lot of coverage in the media. Authors get the same kind of publicity as film stars. It's important to publicize to sell well, but till you sell well you don't have funds to publicize. It's a catch-22 situation. There are hardly any readers in India who would go to a bookshop and buy an untried author. In that respect the Indian readership is still very narrow-minded. So you need to publicize heavily and generate talk about a book. Unless someone had been published in the West and is talked about – then there is a ripple effect.

3.   What have been your output and stand as far as translations from regional languages into English are concerned?

We don't have very systematic programs of translation, like Katha or Macmillan. We do publish some translations, about 6-7 good translations every year. Much as we would like to, our output of regional translations has not been very concerted. For the current year, we plan to bring six translations. We at Rupa and HarperCollins have always been interested in translations.

4.   Then why is the output meagre? Is it not an economically viable to publish translations?

They sell well here. There is very little market abroad. The west is interested only in contemporary fiction in English. Even the best of translations, such as Satyajit Ray's Appu Trilogy does not do well in the West. As far as financial returns go, non-fiction sells the most (biographies, autobiographies).

The problem perennially is getting good translations. English is a problem. It's difficult to find people who write well in English. This applies to Indian

English writing as well as ILEt. I think the standards of English have gone down drastically.

5.   Is there any system by which you select translations?
Since translations are such a small part of our entire list, we don't go about it in the best possible manner. Ideally there should be an editor acquainted with what is happening in regional literatures. At the moment my colleague and I commission translations if we have heard about something from say Bengali, Sanskrit or any of the South Indian languages. This also means that we can produce translations from languages that in-house editors know, which is always limited.

6.   What kind of translations do you produce?
We publish translations at two levels – classics and contemporary literature. There is always a market for classics – amongst students, academic circles, and general readers. There is a generation of people which wants to read its classics since it was not exposed to these books when growing up. I am talking of our generation, which grew up on British texts and now wants to read the Indian stuff. As far as the next generation goes, for all you know they may not read at all. But if there is body of regional writing in good translation, they will surely be attracted to it.

Kali for Women

It is one of the biggest feminist publishing houses in India. Established in 1984, Kali has striven to link political feminism and scholarship in a number of ways. One of the activities at Kali is to foreground through English, women's voices from regional literature, especially writing that interrogates the patriarchal structures of its time. Kali publishes important work previously unavailable in English, or reissues work that may have been translated but is offered afresh in a new translation that reveals other aspects of the original. I have presented below an interview with Urvashi Butalia, the co-founder of Kali for Women. The interview was taken on 26 December, 1997.

1.   Has there been a rise in English-language books?
It is difficult to know accurately if there is a rise in the actual number of books. There is certainly a rise in visibility. It is difficult to know accurately because there are no systems of knowing. But there are certain conditions, certain critical developments as a result of which it is entirely possible that there is some change. The cause of this is the devaluation of the rupee against the dollar some years ago. What that meant was that India was one of the largest markets for imported books, for the US and UK. But with the fall in the rupee even the cheapest of imported books, even remainders, were doubled in price. There was some kind of gap – a space, a horribly small space taken by Indian publishers.

   The development of Indian publishing in English, particularly of Indian books geared towards the individual reader (who was always inconsequential) developed. Till now the bulk of books were educational books. All sales were library sales.

The 'lessening of imported books' and a rise of trade books has grown in tandem with the economic changes. Penguin started Trade books and then Kali, Ravidayal – all these are very visible because there is a great amount of time and effort spent in promoting them.

2.   Are there better promoting systems?
There are now more review journals. Magazines carry extracts and actually pay for them. There is much more talk about books.

3.   Do you think there is a change in reading habits today? People want to
     read more Indian books?
Again it's difficult to say – it does seem that people are reading more and about Indian authors. The sales figures of Arundhati Roy are 50,000 (hardcover) and five years ago, Vikram Seth's *Suitable Boy* was 12,000 in hardcover. The sales seem to show that people are purchasing books even if they don't read them. Lets hope that they do read them. What is happening is that books are being made into desirable objects. The visibilizing of book has a direct impact on purchasing. That's nice. But what it means is that only those books on which you spend money results in sales, the rest fall by the wayside. That is unfortunate. We will lose a lot of good stuff.

4.   Tell me more about Kali. Do you publish only in English?
No we publish in Hindi as well. There are definitely ideological implications to English. But our training as publishers has been in English language publishing. So we do the next best thing. We work with publishers who deal with Indian languages, NGOs etc. The whole structure in Indian languages is so different, pricing etc. In business terms it makes sense to work in English even if ideologically we are committed to other languages. It is a matter of some regret.

5.   What are your modes of distribution?
We have very close contacts with NGOs. Apart from that normal channels like mailing lists, wholesalers. In a sense we are lucky. Whatever we do it's from our office. We are too small to have representatives travelling all over. But our books kind of sell themselves. If we worked harder at selling them, our sales would be double or treble. So far we have managed to keep our head above water.

6.   What are your means of uniform representation?
We go by personal recommendations. If someone draws our attention to some author we ask for a synopsis of a story or a novel.

Orient Longman

O.L Ltd. is the oldest former British publisher in the country. Longman Green set up in the 1880s. The present company became independent in 1948, starting with school, then with college textbooks. Longman is still a minority shareholder, whose titles are stocked and distributed and, in some cases, reprinted. The interview below held on 9 May, 1998 is with V. Abdulla, former editor at Orient Longman.

1. Does O.L have a completely Indian ownership? What is its relationship with O.L abroad?

Orient Longman is an affiliate of the original Longman Green & Co. Ltd., a British publishing house of more than hundred and fifty years' standing. The original company is now defunct, having got itself merged with some British Publishing unit connected with the Financial Times who own Penguin as well. O.L. was incorporated in 1947 after Indian Independence and two third shareholding is controlled by Indians. It has always been associated with the British publishing group which brought it into being. I cannot now say whether a tenuous connection exists as the 'grandfather' itself/himself has lost its corporate identity.

2. What has been the publishing thrust of O.L? Over the years has its emphasis shifted from educational to trade books?

The publishing thrust of O.L. over the years has been educational, basically E.L.T., which was more or less controlled by the British giants, Macmillans, OUP, O.L itself and Blackies. This stranglehold is now gone for good. But trade books do take up a considerable space in the O.L catalogues.

3. What were the features of Orient Paperbacks? When did it come about?

'Orient Paperbacks' is the logo of a small Bombay Publishing company, I don't remember which; I wonder if it still exists now.

4. What role have translations played in the publishing scheme at OL?

Translations from Indian Language fiction into English became part of the O.L. publishing programme only after they adopted the Sangam imprint, some time during the mid seventies. I can tell you it was far from viable at its inception.

5. Was translation a viable business in the 60s-70s when the Sangam series was brought out?

I can tell you that in those days when Dr. Sujit Mukherji and I slogged at the English translations, he from Bengali, and I from Malyalam, I do not remember our royalty having ever reached three-digit figures. Things are different now when leading English publishing units in India have realized the wealth of creative material in Indian languages and translations find a ready market in India and abroad.

6. What happened to the Sangam series? What relationship has it had with Disha books?

The Sangam series started round about the 70's and was wound up by the parent company when they started using it as an emblem for their U.K unit. Then 'Disha' came into being. Now the old 'Sangam' books have taken a new 'avatara' as Disha in India.

7. Many publishers are interested in producing English translations of regional literatures. What social, economic and cultural reasons underlie this change?

The recent tendency, especially in the nineties, for Indian publishers in bringing out English translations of original writing in Indian languages is a sign of the increasing awareness of their importance and vitality in Indian creative writing. This idea of translating from original writing in Indian languages had been part of the ideals of the various state Sahitya Akademis, inspired by Nehru, but they remained just paper aspirations till now. Another reason perhaps is that what is now called 'Comparative Literature' in the syllabi of Indian universities has started becoming an active focus of studies these days. By and large there is no doubt that Indian writing in Indian languages has an 'earthiness' and 'an Indian soul' that are found lacking in what is called 'Indo-Anglian' writing.

Stree

Stree and Samya are two imprints of a partnership between Mandira Sen and Popular Prakashan. Stree's main focus is gender issues while Samya looks at issues of caste and social inequality and aims at giving dalits and Other Backward Castes a published voice. Both imprints by to examine the dynamism of knowledge and the processes through which knowledge acquires legitimacy. Given below is an interview with Mandira Sen conducted on 9 June, 2001.

1. Do you as a part of Samya/Stree team publish translations? If yes, what is the percentage of translations of your total output?

Yes, Stree and Samya do publish translation. Stree has a programme called informally 'literature in translation' and this does about 10-15 per cent of our output. It is hard to quantify because these translations are in the works for about 3 years before they come out. So while the publications of a particular year may not show a translation, the editorial programme has them as ongoing ones. Stree's first book was a translation from Marathi of the fictionalized biography of Anandi Bai Joshi, India's first woman doctor. It was called *Anandi Gopal*. Stree also publishes women's studies in Bengali. These are original works. Kali for Women wants to translate a piece from one of our Bengali books in an anthology on widows.

Samya is just starting to do translations. We believe we do need to present personal stories of the dalits and OBCs. This means translating from a regional language to English, for instance, we are publishing Omprakash Valmiki's *Joothan* in English. The translations into our regional languages of any of our published books are sometimes handled by us, i.e. we organize them because we are anxious about the quality. But we do not publish them because we do not have the expertise and would not be able to handle distribution. So we make a royalty arrangement with a publisher in the particular language group. There may be more translations in Samya, we see this as a growth area.

2. What kind of works in English translation do you produce? What is the criterion of selection? Do you have any mechanism of testing quality?

The translations in Stree have usually been fiction, to show women's contribution to literature. Susie Tharu, our series editor in the '*Gender, Culture, Politics*' series, actively scouts round for quality fiction. This is how Kamal Desai, *The Dark Sun and The Woman Who Wore a Hat* (Marathi), Lalithambika Antherjanam, *Cast Me Out If You Will: Stories and Memoir* (Malayalam) and Saroj Pathak, *Whom Can I Tell? How Can I Explain?* (Gujarati) has come to us. We can handle, as you would expect, the Bengali ourselves, though one we have place in this series; Sulekha Sanyal: *Chhobi*. We published Jyotirmoyee Devi, *The Impermanence of Lies*, a selection of her short stories,and Ganguly and Dutta Gupta, *The Stream Within: Short Stories by Contemporary Bengali Women* – including Bangladeshis. We can handle translationsfrom Marathi because our business partners are Popular Prakashan of Mumbai, with a very high quality Marathi Literature list. They told us about the Anandi Gopal book and we also got *Kharamaster* by Vibhavari Shirurkar through them. Stree published its first nonfiction translation this year: *In Search of Freedom: An Unfinished Journey* by Manikuntala Sen. The original book was in Bengali, written about 20 years ago. Manikuntala was an early communist woman of old East Bengal (today's Bangladesh). She joined the Communist movement when she was about 19, rose to be the deputy leader of the Opposition in the WB Legislature when Jyoti Basu was the leader. Then disgusted with the self-serving, the corruption, the refusal to grant more space to women, she just left.

3. Mechanism for testing quality of the original?

Someone knowledgeable has to read it and advice. Quality of the English translation, we have to set this ourselves.

4. What has been the market for books published by your firm? What has been the reception of works-in-translation?

We are not as strong as we should be. The books do ok, in the sense they sell out in two years or so, the reprint takes longer. It is hard to fight for shelf space with foreign books. Translations, despite the Crossword award, still do now have the 'glamour' of writing in English by Indians, though often, as you know, these are of indifferent quality. We failed to market a very sensitive translation of Anna Akhmatova directly into Bengali. It is a marvellous book but ahead of its time for the market. We are now trying to promote the translations more vigourously – mailing, exhibitions, and so on.

5.   What is the publishing profile of your firm like?
Our publishing profile can be described as high quality, academic, scholarly, and is summed up in the word 'niche', of women's studies. Our books travel abroad.Thus the translations are also seen specialized, quality, we can't handle more popular material.

6. What are the origins and focus of Stree? (I am equally interested in your
     imprints like Samya).
Both are imprints of a partnership of Popular Pakashan and myself. We are professionals. Popular Prakashan was founded in 1924; published Kosambi, Ghurye, A R Desai, medical books, Marathi literature. I trained in publishing in the USA, from the bottom up, if you like. We were interested in using the new conceptual tools that had transformed the social sciences in the seventies, which were directly a result of the women's movement, to see how women's conditionin India could be analyzed. Knowledge itself, the way you looked at issues and institutions, perceptions, were all changing. Samya was founded by us because we wanted to see what social changes, especially of caste, were doing to the lives of these very castes. Also to examine how knowledge is created, what gets legitimacy and so forth.

7.   Do you think there is a greater market for English books today? What do
     you attribute this to?
A greater market for English; yes, indeed. More education; and it is the language of status and power. Moreover the old elite that used to read in its mother tongue too has given way to elites which maybe just use the mother tongues verbally; serious portend for their future. Today's so-called educated thinks it is chic just to handle everything in English. There is the illusion this links them with the centres of 'power and action' abroad; to a certain extend, it does.

8.   What has been the effect of liberalization post 1991 in the publishing
     industry?
Some foreign firms have formed subsidiaries. Penguin already existed but now you saw HarperCollins, Picador India. Maybe some literary agents keep con-tacts with India. Dorling Kindersley works as an outsourcer for its foreign houses in the UK, producing books in India for markets in the UK and USA (they employ elite women whom they pay the highest rates in publishing in India, but which are still cheap compared to labour costs in the UK). Outsourcing may increase. But so far the print media is still protected. Many more Indian startups have taken place.

9. What is the pattern of distribution in India? What are the margins at various levels?

You have to do this through regional distributors. And the discounts tend to be 45-50 per cent. Then within your area you have other local distributors and retailers. Discounts and credit terms remain the same. And books are sold on at least 90 days credit, more like 120 days credit, often 180 days credit and can be returned to you unsold too. This is the standard pattern all over the world (abroad there are places with no fixed price either). You have to have sales people travelling and keeping in touch with distributors. You have to extract the money owed you too; almost no one sends this automatically.

10. Do you import books? Can you give me some facts about your domestic and international market?

No we do not import books. Our domestic market is our major market. We prefer to handle foreign markets by selling rights to a foreign publisher, whereby that book becomes their book and enters their editorial and distributive networks. We have got ourselves a distributor in the UK for the first time to cover UK and Europe.

11. Approximately how many books do you publish annually?
We publish about 7-8 books annually.

12. When did you first publish a translated work in India? Title.
1992. Anandi Gopal (from the Marathi).

13. Is publishing Indian literature in English translation an economically viable business for you?
Just about, on its own, but if we sell rights abroad then its even better!

14. What are the rates of payment as far as translators are concerned? Do they have copyrights?

There are various arrangements. Sometimes translators have got a lump sum payment. If they have worked on an entire book, then they do get the copyright of the translation and are put on a royalty basis (the publisher has to pay the original copyright holder also).

15. How does the hierarchy in the tripartite scheme of publisher-writer-translator operate?

You have to work as a team. Usually the original writer has to be kept placated and shown what is translated. If the translator is very able, then the publisher doesn't have to do that much. It is hard to find good translators. Most people feel that they know two languages and are thus competent. Doesn't work like that. A number of drafts are called for. Always have to keep the potential reader in mind. If there is any problem it generally has to be handled by the publisher.

This is true for any book, really. When something is sorted out editorially for any author, it makes sense to show it is the author's book and can only be passed with her/hiscooperation.

15. What percentage or units of books are exported abroad and to whom? Is there a market? What percentage of books exported abroad?
I take this is for us. See no 10. About 30 percent of our titles. Again, our marketing is being revamped. You have to process the translated text with the foreign publishers. Indian agents abroad prefer 'best sellers'. They aren't keen on translations, but if you tie up with a foreign firm, that is another matter. Also, it depends whom you are translating. I suspect the Oxford Tagores will go well. Also anything by Mahasweta Devi! So yes, the foreign market is chancy.

Bibliography

Ahmad, A. (1994) *In Theory: Classes, Nations, Literatures*. Delhi: Oxford UP.

Altbach, P. (1975) *Publishing in India: An Analysis*. Delhi: Oxford UP.

Aronson, A. (1943) *Rabindranath Through Western Eyes*. Allahabad: Kitabistan.

Aschcroft, B., *et al.* (1989) *The Empire Writes Back: Theory and Practice in Postcolonial Literatures*. London: Routledge.

------ (ed.) (1995) *The Post-Colonial Studies Reader.* London: Routledge.

Baker, M. (gen. ed.) (1998) Routledge *Encylopedia of Translation Studies*. London: Routledge.

Bassnett, S. (ed.) (1991) *Translation Studies*. London: Routledge.

------ and A. Lefevere (eds.) (1990) *Translation, History and Culture*. London: Pinter Publishers.

Breckenridge, Carol A. and Peter van der Meer (eds.) (1993) *Orientalism and the Postcolonial Predicament: Perspectives on South Asia*. Philadelphia: University of Pennsylvania.

Brennan, T. (1989) *Salman Rushdie and the Third World: Myths of the Nation.* New York: St. Martin's Press.

Brower, R. (ed.) (1966) *On Translation.* New York: Oxford UP.

Catford, J.C. (1965) *A Linguistic Theory of Translation*. London: Oxford UP.

Chaudhury, S. (1999) *Translation and Understanding*. Delhi: OUP.

Chavda, V. S. (n.d.) *Modern Gujarat*. Ahmedabad: New Order Book Company.

Cheyfitz, E. (1991) *The Poetic of Imperialism: Translation and Colonization from The Tempest to Tarzan*. New York: Oxford UP.

Chitnis, S. and A. Philip (eds.) (1993) *Higher Education Reform in India: Experience and Perspectives*. New Delhi: Sage Publications.

Cohn, B. (1996) *Colonialism and its Forms of Knowledge: The British in India*. Princeton UP.

Clifford, J. and G. Marcus (eds.) (1986) *Writing Culture: The Poetics and Politics of Ethnography.* Berkeley and Los Angeles: University of California Press.

Das, S. K. (1991) *A History of Indian Literature: Western Impact: Indian Response 1800 -1910*. Delhi: Sahitya Akademi.

------ (1994) *The English Writings of Rabindranath Tagore: Poetry.* Delhi: Sahitya Akademi.

------ (1995) *A History of Indian Literature: Triumph and Tragedy 1911-1956.* Delhi: Sahtiya Akademi.

Devy, G.N. (1992) *After Amnesia*. Hyderabad: Orient Longman.

------ (1993) *In Another Tongue: Essays on Indian English Literature*. Madras: Macmillan India.

------ (1998) *Of Many Heroes: An Indian Essay in Literary Historiography.* Mumbai: Orient Longman.

Dingwaney, A. and C. Maier (eds.) (1996) *Between Languages and Cultures*. Delhi: Oxford UP.

Drew, J. (1987) *India and the Romantic Imagination*. India: Oxford UP.

Gokak, V.K. (1964) *English in India: Its Present and Future*. Bombay: Asia Publishing House.

Hermans, T. (ed.) (1985) *The Manipulation of Literature*. London: Croom Helm.

Homel, D. and S. Simon (1988) *Mapping Literature: The Art and Politics of Translation*. Montreal: Vehicle Press.

Iyengar, K.R.S. (1985) *Indian Writing in English*. New Delhi: Sterling Publishers.

Jhaveri, K.M. (1914) *Milestones in Gujarati Literature*. Gujarat.

Jhaveri, M. (1976) *History of Gujarati Literature*. Delhi: Sahitya Akademi.

Joshi, U. (1990) *The Idea of Indian Literature, Samvatsar Lectures*. Delhi: Sahitya Akademi.

Joshi, Y. (1992). *The English Writings in Gujarat 1750-1850*. Unpublished Dissertation Gujarat University.

Kachru, B. (ed.) (1982) *The Other Tongue: English Across Cultures*. Urbana: University of Illinois Press.

Kesavan, B.S. (1985) *The History of Printing and Publishing: A Story of Cultural Awakening*, 3 vols. Delhi: National Book Trust.

Khilnani, S. (1997) *The Idea of India*. London: Hamish Hamilton.

Khubchandani, L. (1991) *Language Culture and Nation Building:Challenges of Modernisation*. Shimla: IIAS and New Delhi: Manohar Publications.

King, B. (ed.) (1996) *New National and Post-Colonial Literatures: An Introduction*. Oxford: Clarendon Press.

King, R.D. (1997) *Nehru and the Language Politics of India*. Delhi: OUP.

Kopf, D. (1969) *British Orientalism and the Bengal Renaissance: The Dynamics of Indian Modernization, 1773 – 1835*. Berkeley and Los Angeles: University of California Press.

Krishna, S. (1991) *India's Living Languages*. Delhi: Allied Publishers.

Krishnaswamy, N. and A. Burde (1998) *The Politics of Indians' English: Linguistic Colonialism and the Expanding English Empire*. Delhi: Oxford UP.

Kulkarni, V.B. (1951) *British Statesmen in India*. India: Orient Longman.

Kumar, N. (1998) *India:50 years of Independence, Publishing*. Delhi: B.R. Publishing Corporation.

Lawson, P. (1993) *The East India Company: A History*. London: Longman.

Lefevre, A. (1992a) *Translation, Rewriting, and the Manipulation of Literary Fame*. London and New York: Routledge.

------ (ed. and trans.) (1992b) *Translation/History/Culture: A Sourcebook*. London and New York: Routledge.

Loomba, A. (1998) *Colonialism/Postcolonialism*. London: Routledge.

Malhotra, D.N. (ed.) (1998) *50 years of book publishing in India since Independence*. Delhi: The Federation of Indian Publishers.

Marshall, P.J. (ed.) (1970) *The British Discovery of Hinduism in the Eighteenth Century*. London: Cambridge UP.

Majeed, J. (1992) *Ungoverned Imaginings: James Mill's The History of British India and Orientalism*. Oxford: Clarendon Press.

Maniar, U.M. (1969) *The Influence of English on Gujarati Poetry*. Unpublished Dissertation: M.S.University of Baroda.

Metcalf, T. (1995) *Ideologies of the Raj. The New Cambridge History of India*. London: Cambridge U P.

Mill, J. (ed.) (1858) *The History of British India*. London: H.H. Wilson.

Mohanty, J.M. (compiled) (1984) *Indian Literature in English Translation: A Bibliography.* Mysore: Central Institute of Indian Languages.

Mongia P. (ed.) (1997) *Contemporary Postcolononial Theory: A Reader.* Delhi: Oxford UP.

Morley, D. and K. Robins (1995) *Spaces of Identity: global media, electronic landscapes and cultural boundaries.* London: Routledge.

Mukherjee, K. (1955) *Reorganisation of Indian States.* Bombay: Popular Prakashan.

Mukherjee, M. (ed.) (1985) *Realism and Reality: The Novel and Society in India.* Delhi: Oxford U P.

Mukherjee, M. (2000) *The Perishable Empire.* New Delhi: Oxford UP.

Mukherjee, S. (1975) *Towards a Literary History of India.* Shimla: Indian Institute of Advanced Study.

------ (rev. ed.) (1994) *Translation as Discovery.* Hyderabad: Orient Longman.

Mukherjee, T. (1998) *Translation: From Periphery to Centrestage.* New Delhi: Prestige Books.

Naik, M.K (1982) *A History of Indian English Literature.* Delhi: Sahitya Akademi.

Nair, R. B. (ed.) (2002) *Translation, Text and Theory: The Paradigm of India.* New Delhi: Sage Publication and London: Thousand Oaks.

Nandy, A. (1983) *The Intimate Enemy:Loss and Recovery of Self under Colonialism.* Delhi: Oxford UP.

------ (1990) *At the Edge of Psychology.* Delhi: Oxford U P.

Narasimhaiah, C.D. (1969) *The Swan and the Eagle.* Simla: Indian Institute of Advanced Study.

Niranjana, T. (1992) *Sitting Translation: History, Post-Structuralism, and the Colonial Context.* Hyderabad: Orient Longman.

Panikkar, K.N. (1995) *Culture, Ideology, Hegemony: Intellectuals and Social Consciousness in Colonial India.* Delhi: Tulika.

Paniker, A. (ed.) (1992) *Making of Indian Literature: A Consolidated Report of Workshops on Literary Translations 1986-1988.* New Delhi: Sahitya Akademi.

Parekh, H .T. (1932) *Gujarat Vernacular Society nun Itihas (The History of the Gujarat Vernacular Society).* 3 vols. Ahmedabad.

Patel, C.N. (1986) *Moral and Social Thinking in Gujarat.* Gandhinagar: Gujarat Sahitya Akademi.

Patel, M. (1959) *Mahatma Gandhi ni Kelavni Philsuphi (Mahatma Gandhi's Philosophy of Education).* Ahmedabad: Navjivan Prakashan Mandir.

Podder, R.A. (1972) *Indian Literature.* Shimla: Indian Institute of Advanced Study.

Rao, D.S. (1985) *A Short History of Sahitya Akademi 1954-84.* Delhi: Sahitya Akademi.

Ramakrishna, S. (ed.) (1997) *Translation and Multinlingualism: Post- colonial Contexts.* Delhi: Pencraft International.

Rangarajan, T. (1986) *Research Projects on Educational Standards in Gujarat: Final Report.* Ahmedabad: Vikram Sarabhai Memorial Trust.

Robertson, B.C. (1995) *Rammohun Roy:The Father of Modern India.* Delhi: Oxford UP.

Robinson, D. (1997) *Translation and Empire: Postcolonial Theories Explained.* Manchester: St.Jerome.

Rocher, R. (1983) *Orientalism, Poetry, and the Millenium: The Checkered Life of Nathaniel B. Halhed 1751-1830*. Delhi: Motilal Banarsidas.

Rose, M. (ed.) (1981) *Translation Spectrum: Essays in Theory and Practice*. Albany: State University of New York Press.

Said, E. (1979) *Orientalism* New York: Vintage Books.

Schulte, R. and J. Biguenet (eds) (1992) *Theories of Translation: An Anthology of Essays from Dryden to Derrida*. Chicago: The University of Chicago Press.

Seervai, H.M. (1984) *Constitutional Law of India: A Critical Commentary*. Bombay: N.M Tripathi and London: Sweet and Maxwell, 3rd ed.

Simon, S. (1996) *Gender in Translation*. New York: Routledge.

Singh, A. (ed.) (1996) *Translation: Its Theory and Practice*. New Delhi: Creative Books.

Singh, J. (1996) *Colonial Narratives/Cultural Dialogues*. London: Routledge.

Society Under Siege, Seminar (513), May, 2002.

Spivak, G.C. (1993) *Outside in the Teaching Machine*. New York: Routledge.

Toury, G. (1998) *Translation Across Cultures*. New Delhi: Bahri Publishers.

Trivedi, H. (1993) *Colonial Transactions: English Literature and India*. Calcutta: Papyrus.

Varma, P. (1998) *The Great Indian Middle Class*. Delhi: Viking Penguin India.

Venuti, L. (ed.) (1992) *Rethinking Translation: Discourse, Subjectivity, Ideology*. New York & London: Routledge.

------ (1995) *The Translator's Invisibility*. New York & London: Routledge.

Viswanathan, G. (1989) *Masks of Conquest: Literary Study and British Rule in India*. London: Faber.

Works Sited

Abdulla, V. (Sept-Nov 1995) Problems of Interpretation. *Indian Review of Books*.

Aggarwal, J.C. (1993) *Landmarks in the History of Modern Indian Education*. New Delhi: Vikas Publishing House.

Ahmad, A. (1994) *In Theory: Classes, Nations, Literatures*. Delhi: Oxford U P.

Altbach, P. (1975) *Publishing in India: An Analysis*. Delhi: Oxford U P.

Ambedkar, B. R. (1992) in Verinder Grover (ed), *Political Thinkers of Modern India – Vol.-XVI*. Delhi: Deep and Deep Publishers.

Aronson, A. (1943) *Rabindranath through Western Eyes*. Allahabad: Kitabistan.

Asad, T. (1986) The Concept of Cultural Translation in British Social Anthropology, in James Clifford and George E. Marcus (eds.), *Writing Culture: The Poetics and Politics of Ethnography*, p141-164. Berkeley: University of California Press.

Ashcroft, B., G. Griffiths, and H. Tiffins, (1989) (eds.), *The Empire Writes Back: Theory and Practice in Postcolonial Literatures*. London: Routledge.

Baker, M. (1998) general editor, *Routledge Encyclopedia of Translation Studies*. London: Routledge.

Bassnett, S. ((1980) 1991) (revised edition) *Translation Studies*. London and New York: Routledge.

------ and H. Trivedi, (1999) (eds.) *Postcolonial Translation: Theory and Practice*. London and New York: Routledge.

Bellos, D. (1997) Our Own and Other Tongue, in A.S. Byatt and Peter Porter (eds.) *New Writing 6*. London: Vintage in association with the British Council.

Bhabha, H. (1994) *The Location of Culture*. London: Routledge.

Bhagat, N. (1st October, 1974) Aa Angrezinun te shun karvun (What do we do about this English?) *Jansatta*

Bharucha, R. (2000) Thinking Through Culture: A Perspective for the Millenium, p66-84, in Romila Thapar (ed.), *India Another Millenium?* Delhi: Viking.

Bhave, S. (April 2001) Anuvad: Gaya be varsh nan sahitya nun Sarvainyun (Translation: A survey of the last two years) 107-127 *Parab*.

Blackwood's Edinburgh Magazine Vol. VI, 1820 (Oct. 1819-Mar. 1820).

Brough, J. (1968) Introduction, *Poems from the Sanskrit*. Translated by John Brough. London: Penguin U.K.

Burde, A. and N. Krishnaswamy, (1998) *The Politics of Indians' English: Linguistic Colonialism and the Expanding English Empire*. Delhi: Oxford U P.

Catford, J. C. (1965) *A Linguistic Theory of Translation*. London: Oxford U P.

Chamberlain, L. (2000) Gender and the Metaphorics of Translation, in Lawrence Venuti (ed.), *The Translation Studies Reader*. London and New York: Routledge.

Chaudhuri, J. S. (1994) *Anugandhi Yug nun Anuvaad Sahitya: Ek Sarvekshan (Literary Translation of the post-Gandhian Era: A Survey)*, (unpublished dissertation). Ahmedabad: Gujarat Vidyapeeth.

Chaudhuri I. N. (1998) Publishing of Translations, in D.N. Malhotra (ed.) *Fifty Years of Book Publishing in India since Independence* (182-189). New Delhi: The Federation of Indian Publishers.

Chavda, V.S. (n.d.) *Modern Gujarat*. Ahmedabad: New Order Book Company.

Cheyfitz, E. (1991) *The Poetic of Imperialism: Translation and Colonization from the Tempest to Tarzan.* New York: Oxford U P.

Cohn, B. (1996) *Colonialism and its Forms of Knowledge: The British in India.* New Jersey: Princeton U P.

Das, G. (2000) *India Unbound.* New Delhi: Viking.

Das, S.K. (1991) *A History of Indian Literature: Western Impact: Indian Response 1800-1910* (Vol.VIII). Delhi: Sahitya Akademi.

------ (1994) Introduction, *The English Writings of Rabindranath Tagore: Poetry.* New Delhi: Sahitya Akademi.

------ (1995) *A History of Indian English Literature: Triumph and Tragedy 1911-1950.* Delhi: Sahitya Akademi.

------ (1998) Muses in Isolation, in Amiya Dev and S. K. Das (eds.), *Comparative Literature: Theory and Practice.* Shimla: Indian Institute of Advanced Study.

Dasgupta, P. (15th April, 2000) Sanskrit, English and Dalits. *Economic and Political Weekly*, Mumbai, 1407-1411.

Davidar, D. (29th December 1992) quoted in Makarand Paranjpe: Everyone Seems to have a Novel Ready for Publication, *The Economic Times.*

Dayal, R. (June 1998) Interface: A Dialogue. *The Book Review* XXII: 6, 30-35.

Delisle, J. and J. Woodsworth (eds.) (1995) *Translators through History.* Amsterdam/philadelphia: John Benjamin.

Desai, M. P. (1964) *The Problem of English.* Ahmedabad: Navjivan Publishing House.

Deshpande, S. (4th June 2000) At the Crossroads. *Literary Review.*

Devasia, A. and S. Tharu (1995) Englishing Indulekha: Translation, the Novel and History. *Haritham* 5-23.

Devi, M. (1995) *Imaginary Maps*, translated by Gayatri Spivak. London and New York: Routledge.

Devy, G.N. (1992) *After Amnesia: Tradition and Change in Indian Literary Criticism.* Bombay: Orient Longman.

------ (1993) *In Another Tongue: Essays on Indian English Literature.* Madras: Macmillan India.

------ (1998a) *Of Many Heroes: An Indian Essay in Historiography.* Mumbai: Orient Longman.

------ (1998b) Foreword, *Adivasi Communities and Languages of India.* Nima Gadhia (ed.) Baroda: Bhasha Research and Publication Centre.

------ (2002) (ed.) *Painted Words: An Anthology of Tribal Literature.* New Delhi: Penguin Books

Dharamarajan, G. (1998) Introduction, *Separate Journeys: Stories by Women.* New Delhi: Katha and Garutman.

Dharwadkar, A. and V. Dharwadkar (1997) Indian English Literature: Literature and Commercial Success, in V. N. Narayanan and Jyoti Sabharwal (eds.), *India at 50: Bliss of Hope and Burden of Reality,* 247-262. Delhi: Sterling Publishers.

Dharwadkar, V. (1994) Postcolonial Cosmopolitanism: A Note on A.K. Ramanujan's Theory and Practice of Criticism and Translation. *Indian Literature 37:2,* 91-97.

Drew, J. (1987) *India and the Romantic Imagination.* Delhi: Oxford U P.

D'Souza, P. quoted in Rustom Bharucha, Thinking Through Culture: A Perspective for the Millenium, 66-84, in Romila Thapar (ed.), *India Another Millenium?*

(2000). Delhi: Viking.

Dutt, M.M. ((1859) 1965) (trans.) *Marriage of Hindu Widows and Sermista,* in M. Racanabali (ed.) Ksetra Gupta, Sahitya Samsad. Calcutta .

Dutt, R.C. ((1877) 1895) *The Literature of Bengal.* Calcutta: Thacker Spinck and Co.

------ (1889) *A History of Civilization in Ancient India.*

------ (1903) *The Economic History of India.* Publication Division: India.

------ (1910) 1929) Translator's Epilogue, *The Ramayana and Mahabharata condensed into English.* London (1910): J.M. Dent and Sons (1929).

Evan-Zohar, I. (1998) The Position of Translated Literature within the Literary Polysystem, in G. Toury (ed.), *Translation Across Cultures,* 109-117. Delhi: Bahri Publications. Also in L. Venuti (ed.), *The Translation Studies Reader* (2000). London and New York: Routledge.

Forbes, D. (1859) (trans.) *Mir Amman's Bagh O Bahar. London*

Gandhi, M. K. (1928) *Young India.*

------ (9 August 1938). *Harijan.*

------ ((1946) 1995) Foreword, *The Gospel of Selfless Action or The Gita, According to Gandhi,* translated by M.P. Desai. Ahmedabad: Navjivan Publishing House.

------ (1953) *Towards New Education.* Ahmedabad: Navjivan Publishing House.

Gangadhar, V. (14th January 2001) Needed: A Linguistic Awakening. *The Hindu.*

Ghosh, J. (13th Aug 1999) The International Culture Trade. *Frontline,* 106-107.

Godard, B. (1986) Translator's Preface, in N. Brossard, *Lovers.* Montreal: Guernica.

Gokak, V.K. (1964) *English in India: Its Present and Future.* Bombay: Asia Publishing House.

Grady, S.G. (1869) Editor's Note, *Institutes of Hindu Law or the Ordinances of Menu,* trans., William Jones, 3rd ed. London: W. H. Allen & Co.

Guha, S. (23th March 1997) English Please, We're Indian. *The Express Magazine.*

Gupta, S.S. (1972) Introduction, in Dinabandhu Mitra, *Nil Durpan, or the Indigo Planting Mirror, Translated by a Native.* Calcutta: Indian Publications.

Halhed, N.B. (1970) 'The Translator's Preface' to *A Code of Gentoo Laws,* in P.J. Marshall (ed.) *The British Discovery of Hinduism in the Eighteenth Century.* London: Cambridge U P.

Hassan, A. (Sept-Nov 1995) The North-East: A Tale of Two Literatures. *Indian Review of Books,* 26-30.

Hastings, W. (1970) 'Letter to Nathaniel Smith', from *The Bhagvat-Geeta,* in P.J. Marshall (ed.), *The British Discovery of Hinduism in the Eighteenth Century.* London: Cambridge U P.

Hermans, T. (ed.) (1985) *The Manipulation of Literature: Studies in Literary Translation.* London: Croom Helm.

Hochshild, A. (23th May 1998) *Economic and Political Weekly,* 1235-1238.

Holmstrom, L. (Mar-April 1997) New Maps for the Old. *Indian Review of Books,* p 4-5.

Hume, R. (1934) Introduction, *The Thirteen Principal Upanishads.* Oxford: Oxford U P.

Inden, R. (1986) Orientalist Constructions of India. *Modern Asian Studies 20.*

Jeffrey, R. (18th Sept. 1993) Indian Language Newspapers and Why They Grow. *Economic and Political Weekly.* 2004-2010.

Jeffrey, R. (29th March 1997) Urdu: Waiting for Citizen Kane? *Economic and Politi-*

cal Weekly 631-635.

Jones, W. (1869) Preface, *Institutes of Hindu Law or the Ordinances of Menu,* 3rd ed. London: W. H. Allen &Co.

------ (1970) 1970) On The Hindus, in P.J. Marshall (ed.), *The British Discovery of Hinduism in the Eighteenth Century.* London: Cambridge UP.

------ (1788) Jones to Cornwallis, 19th March 1788, in Garland Cannon, ed., *The Letters of Sir William Jones.* Oxford: Oxford U P.

Joshi, S. (ed.), ((1991) 1992, 2nd ed.) *Rethinking English: Essays in Literature, Language, History.* Delhi: Oxford U P.

Joshi, Y. (1992) *The English Writings in Gujarat 1750-1850* (unpublished dissertation). Ahmedabad: Gujarat Vidyapeeth.

Kapoor, K. (1997) Philosophy of Translation: Subordinatination or Subordinating: translating Technical Texts from Sanskrit – Now and Then, in Shanta Ramakrishna (ed.), *Translation and Multilingualism; Post-Colonial Contexts*, 146-156. Delhi: Pencraft International.

Kaviraj, S. (1992) "Writing, Speaking, Being: Language and the Historical Formation of Identities in India", in Dagmar Hellmann-Rajanayagam and Dietmar Rothermund (eds.), *Nationalstaat und Sprachkonflikte in Sud-und Sudostasien.* Stuttgart: Franz Sterner Verlag.

Kejriwal, O.P. (1988) *The Asiatic Society of Bengal and the Discovery of India's Past 1784-1838.* Delhi: Oxford U P.

Kesavan, B.S. (1985) *The History of Printing and Publishing: A Story of Cultural Awakening* (3 vols.) I. Delhi: National Book Trust.

Khare, H. (October 1998) An Unending Struggle for Gujarat's Political Soul. *Seminar* 470, 17-23.

Khilnani, S. (1997) *The Idea of India.* London: Hamish Hamilton.

Krishna S. (1991) *India's Living Languages: The Critical Issues.* New Delhi: Allied Publishers.

Krishnan, M. (1997) Editor's Preface, Matampu Kunjukuttan's *Outcaste.* Translated by Vasanthi Shankaranarayanan. Delhi: Macmillan India.

Kumar, Nita (translator), Geetanjali Shree's *Mai.* (1997: Hindi, 2000: English Translation). Delhi: Kali for Women.

Kumar, Narendra (1998) *India: 50 years of Independence: Publishing.* Delhi: B.R. Publishing Corporation.

Lago, M. (1986) Tagore in Translation: A Case Study in Literary Exchange. *Indian Literature* 29:3. 416-421.

Lakshmi, C.S. (1997) Anuvad: Linking Literatures. Transcript of a seminar on Translation, *The Book Review* (2 parts) *I.*

Lefevere, A. (2000) Mother Courage's Cucumbers: Text, System and Refraction in a Theory of Literature, in L. Venuti (ed.), *The Translation Studies Reader.* London and New York: Rouledge.

Long, J. (1972) Note. Dinabandhu Mitra's *Nil Durpan, Translated by a Native*, Sankar Sen Gupta (ed.). Calcutta: Indian Publications.

Loomba, A. (1998) *Colonialism/Postcolonialism.* London: Routledge.

Machwe, P. (1979) *Literary Sketches.* Calcutta: Writer's Workshop.

Mahipatram, R.N. ((1866) 1996) (revised ed.) *Saasu Vahu ni ladai* (The fight between a daughter-in-law and mother-in-law). Ahmedabad: Gujarat Sahitya

Akademy.

Majeed, J. (1992) *Ungoverned Imaginings: James Mill's The History of British India and Orientalism*. Oxford: Clarendon Press.

McDonald, P. (8th August, 1997) Beyond the Lionizing. *Times Literary Supplement*.

Mehta, D. (1997) *Paanch dayakan nun Sahityik vikas (Literary Development of the five decades)*. Mumbai: Parichay Trust.

Memon, A. and R. Banerji (1997) Tongue Lashing, *India at 50*. Bombay: Ayaz Memon and Book Quest Publishers.

Menon, R. (Sept-Nov 1995) A Publisher's Viewpoint. *Indian Review of Books* 5:1.

------ (1998) Forward: River of Fire (Aag ka Dariya), trans. Q. Hyder. New Delhi: Kali for Women.

------ (2002) Authorial Submissions: Publishing and Translation, in Rukmini Bhaya Nair (ed.), *Translation, Text and Theory: The Paradigm of India*. Sage Publication: New Delhi, Thousand Oaks: London.

Miller, J. E. (ed.) (2001) Introduction, *Who's Who in Contemporary Women's Writing*. London and New York: Routledge.

Mills, J. (1858) in H.H. Wilson (ed.), *The History of British India*. London.

Mitchell, W.J.T. (1995) Postcolonial Culture, Postimperial Criticism, in Bill Ashcroft, Gareth Griffiths and Helen Tiffin (eds.), *The Post-Colonial Studies Reader*. London: Routledge.

Mukherjee, D. and N. Abhilash (1999) "Out of the Shadows", *The Week*, August 15 (pp. 14-16).

Mukherjee, M. (1992) Mapping Territory: Notes on Framing a Course, in Rajeshwari Sunder Rajan (ed.), *Lie of the Land: English Literary Studies in India*, 229-245. Delhi: Oxford U P.

------ (June 1998) Interface: A Dialogue. *The Book Review* p 30-35.

------ (2000) *The Perishable Empire*. New Delhi: Oxford U P.

Mukherjee, S. (May-June 1991) 'Operation Mahasweta', *The Book Review* XV:3.

------ (1994) *Translation as Discovery*, 2nd ed. Hyderabad: Orient Longman.

------ (1997) Transcreating Translation. *Indian Literature* 40:4,158-167.

Naik, M.K. (1982) *A History of Indian English Literature*. Delhi: Sahitya Akademi.

Nair, R.B. (May 1998) Politics of Translation. *Outlook*.

------ (2002) Introduction, in Rukmini Bhaya Nair (ed.), *Translation, Text and Theory: The Paradigm of India*. Sage Publications: New Delhi, Thousand Oaks: London.

Nandy, A. (1983) *The Intimate Enemy: Loss and Recovery of Self Under Colonialism*. New Delhi: Oxford U P.

Narayan, R.K. (1998) Fifteen Years, in *Jubilee English Reader*. Mumbai: Jay Publishers.

Navalram, (1966, 2nd ed) Narhari Dwarkadas Parikh (ed.) *Navalgranthavali*. Ahmedabad: Gujarat Vidyapith.

Niranjana, T. (1992) *Siting Translation: History, Post-Structuralism and the Colonial Context*. Hyderabad: Orient Longman.

Pande, M. (2000) *My Own Witness*. Delhi: Viking.

Panikkar, K.N. (1995) *Culture, Ideology, Hegemony: Intellectuals and Social Consciousness in Colonial India*. Delhi: Tulika.

Parekh, H.T. (1932) *Gujarat Vernacular Society nun Itihaas (The History of the Gujarat Vernacular Society)* 3 vols, I. Ahmedabad.

Parekh, B. (1997) National Culture and Multiculturism, in K. Thompson (ed.), *Media and Cultural Regulation*. Delhi: Sage Publications.

Patel, M.S. (1959) *Mahatma Gandhi ni Kelavni Philsuphi (Mahatma Gandhi's Philosophy of Education)*. Ahmedabad: Navjivan Prakashan Mandir.

Patel, B. (February 1989) Angrezimaan Gujarati (Gujarati Through English). *Parab*.

------ (Aug 2001) "Aa varash nun Jnanpeeth" (This year's Jnanpeeth). *Parab, 2-5*.

Prasad, G.J.V. (1999) "Writing Translation: The Strange case of the Indian English Novel" (41-57), in *Postcolonial Translation: Theory and Practice*, S. Bassnett and H. Trivedi. London and New York: Routledge.

Rajan, R. S. (1992) Fixing English: Nation, Language, Subject, in Rajeshwari Sunder Rajan (ed.), *The Lie of the Land: English Literary Studies in India*. Delhi: Oxford U P.

------ (25th Feb 2001) Dealing With Anxieties. *The Hindu*.

Ram, N. (2000) The Great Indian Media Bazaar: Emerging Trends and Issues for the Future, 241-292, in Romila Thapar (ed.), *India Another Millenium?* Delhi: Viking.

Ramakrishnan, E.V. (1997) *Making it New: Modernism in Malayalam, Hindi and Marathi*. Shimla: IIAS.

------ (1999) *The Tree of Tongues: An Anthology of Modern Indian Poetry*. Indian Institute of Advanced Study.

Ramanathan S. and R. Kothari (1998) *Modern Gujarati Poetry: A Selection*. Sahitya Akademi, New Delhi.

Ramanujan, A.K. (1967) (trans.), *The Interior Landscape: Love Poems from a Classical Tamil Anthology*. Bloomington: Indiana U P.

------ (1973) (trans.), *Speaking of Siva*. London: Penguin Books.

------ (1991) (trans.), *Folktales from India: A Selection of oral Tales from Twenty-two Languages*. New York: Pantheon Books.

Rangarajan, T. (1986) Final Report. *Research Projects on Educational Standards in Gujarat*. Ahmedabad : Vikram Sarabhai Memorial Trust.

Rao, D.S. (1985) *A Short History of Sahitya Akademi, 1954-84*. New Delhi: Sahitya Akademi.

Rao, R. (1997) Anuvad: Linking Literatures. Transcript of a seminar on Translation, *The Book Review* (2 parts) *I:xxi-3*, 17-31.

Raychaudhuri, T. (1988) *Europe Reconsidered: Perceptions of the West in 19th Century Bengal*. Delhi: Oxford U P.

Ringold, F. (Spring/Summer 1998) Editor's Preface, India: A Wealth of Diversity. Special Issue *Nimrod*.

Ripken, P. (1991) African Literature in the Literary Marketplace Outside Africa, in Hans M. Zell and Mary Jay (eds.), *The African Book Publishing Record*, 289-291. Oxford: Hans Zell Publishers.

Robertson, B.C. (1995) *Rammohun Roy: The Father of Modern India*. Delhi: Oxford UP.

Rocher, R. (1983) *Orientalism, Poetry, and the Millenium: The Checkered Life of Nathaniel B. Halhed 1751-1830*. Delhi: Motilal Banarsidas.

------ (1993) British Orientalism in the Eighteenth Century: The Dialectics of Knowledge and Government, in Carol A. Breckenridge and Peter Van der Meer (eds.),

Orientalism and the Postcolonial Predicament: Perspectives on South Asia. Philadelphia: University of Pennsylvania.

------ Reconstituting South Asian Studies for a Diasporic Age. www.southasia.upenn.edu/html/rocher.html

Roy, R. (1816) Preface, *Translation of an Abridgement of the Vedanta.* Calcutta.

Rushdie, S. (first pub 1983) *Midnight's Children.* Great Britain: John Cape Ltd.

------ (1991) *Imaginary Homelands.* London: Granta Books in association with Penguin India.

------ (23 and 30 June 1997) Damme, This is the Oriental Scene For You. *The New Yorker* Special Fiction Issue.

------ discussed in G.J.V. Prasad, (1999) Writing Translation: The Strange Case of the Indian English Novel, in S. Bassnett and H. Trivedi (eds.), *Post-colonial Translation: Theory and Practice.* London and New York: Routledge.

Sarang, V. (ed.) (1989) Introduction, *Indian English Poetry Since 1950: An Anthology.* Hyderabad: Orient Longman.

Satchinandan, K. 'The Case of a Wounded Literature'. http://www.griffe.com/projects/india/literature/index.html

Satchidanandan, K. (Sept-Oct. 1997) Celebrating Translation. *Indian Literature* 181.

Schulte, R. (1990-91) "Translation and the Publishing World", Translation Review No. 34/35.

Sengupta, M. (1996) Translation as Manipulation: The Power of Images and Images of Power, in A. Dingwaney and C. Maier (eds.), *Between Languages and Cultures.* Delhi: Oxford UP.

Shankari, S. (ed.) (2000) *Knit India Through Literature.* Delhi: Sahitya Akademi.

Sharma, A. (8th Feb1998) India by the Tale. *The Express Magazine.*

Simon, S. (1996) *Gender in Translation: Cultural Identity and the Politics of Transmission.* London and New York: Routledge.

------ and V. Viswanatha (1999) Shifting Grounds of Exchange: B.M. Srikantaiah and Kannada Translation, in S. Bassnett and H. Trivedi (eds.), *Post-colonial Translation: Theory and Practice.* London and New York: Routledge.

Singh, J. (1996) *Colonial Narratives/Cultural Dialogues.* London: Routledge.

Spivak, G.C. (1993) The Politics of Translation, *Outside in the Teaching Machine.* New York: Routledge.

Srinivasraju, S. (20th Aug. 2001) Travel on Two Boats. *Outlook.*

Sturrock, J. (1990) Writing Between the Lines: The Language of Translation. *New Literary History 21,* 993-1013.

Tagore, R. (first published 1913) Prose Translation, *Gitanjali.* Delhi: Macmillan India.

------ quoted in *Rabindranath Tagore: Poet and Dramatist* (1948). London: Oxford UP.

------ (1997) *Gora.* Translated by Sujit Mukherjee. Delhi: Sahitya Akademi.

Tharu, S. and K. Lalitha (1993) Introduction, *Women Writing in India* (2 vols) *I.* New Delhi: Oxford U P.

Tharu, S. (1998) *Subject to Change: Teaching in the Nineties.* New Delhi: Orient Longman.

Thussu, D.K. (2000) The Hinglish Hegemony: The Impact of Western Television on Broadcasting in India, in D. French and M. Richards (eds.), *Television in*

Contemporary India. New Delhi: Sage Publications.

Toury, G. (ed.) (1998) *Translation Across Cultures*. Delhi: Bahri Publications.

------ (2000) The Nature and Role of Norms in Translation, in Lawrence Venuti (ed.), *The Translation Studies Reader*. London and New York: Routledge.

Trivedi, H. (1996) The Politics of Post-Colonial Translation, in A. Singh (ed.), *Translation: Its Theory and Practice*. New Delhi: Creative Books.

Trivedi, V.J. (17 June, 2002) An Anthology of Indian Drama. *The Times of India*, Ahmedadad.

Varma, P.K. (1998) *The Great Indian Middle Class*. New Delhi: Viking.

Venuti, L. (1992) *Rethinking Translation: Discourse, Subjectivity, Ideology*. London and New York: Routledge.

------ (1995) *The Translator's Invisibility*. London and New York: Routledge.

------ (1998) *Scandals of Translation: Towards an Ethic of Difference*. London: Routledge.

------ (ed.) (2000) *The Translation Studies Reader*. London and New York: Routledge.

Verma, N. quoted in D. Mukerjee and N.U. Abhilash 'Out of the Shadows' (15 Aug 1999), p14-18. *The Week*.

Vijayunni, M. (16th July 1999) The Bilingual Scenario in India. *The Hindu*.

Vishwa Hindu Samachar (April 2002) Godhra Hatya Kaand. Ahmedabad.

Viswanathan, G. (1989) *Masks of Conquest: Literary Study and British Rule in India*. London: Faber.

Wilkins, C. (1970) 'The Translator's Preface' from *The Bhagvat-Geeta*, in P.J. Marshall (ed.), *The British Discovery of Hinduism in the Eighteenth Century*. London: Cambridge UP.

Yagnik, A., S.Trivedy, S. Mayaram and A. Nandy (1995) *Creating a Nationality: The Ramjanmabhoomi*. Delhi: Oxford UP.

Index

For Product Safety Concerns and Information please contact our EU
representative GPSR@taylorandfrancis.com
Taylor & Francis Verlag GmbH, Kaufingerstraße 24, 80331 München, Germany